MANY VOICES

TEACHER'S GUIDE

MANY VOICES

TEACHER'S GUIDE

The National
Storytelling Association

THE NATIONAL STORYTELLING PRESS

Jonesborough, Tennessee

Published by the
National Storytelling Press
of the National Storytelling Association
P.O. Box 309 ■ Jonesborough, Tenn. 37659 ■ 800-525-4514

Printed in the United States

99 98 97 96 95   5 4 3 2 1

Director of Publishing: Nell Tsacrios

Editor: Mary C. Weaver
Writer: Mary L. Dennis
Art Director: Jane L. Hillhouse
Design Assistant: Martha V. Jones
Interior Illustration: Eric Layne

ISBN 1-879991-20-9

Contents

v

How to Use This Guide

We've prepared this teacher's guide to help you and your students make the fullest possible use of the 36 stories in *Many Voices: True Tales From America's Past*. The guide was written for the National Storytelling Press by Mary L. Dennis, a former teacher and a professional education and curriculum writer.

As you'll see, this guide includes a two-page lesson to accompany each story in *Many Voices*. The first page of each lesson is for you, the teacher, and contains the following:

- suggested learning objectives
- background information about the story or its subject matter
- initiating activities to engage students in the topic before the story is read or told
- discussion questions—to be used after the telling—that invite students to dig more deeply into the story and its themes and issues
- follow-up activities that encourage further learning.

Many of the lessons also include brief lists of new words to learn and the storytellers' own tips for telling the tale or enhancing the learning experience.

The second page of each lesson, the activity sheet, is intended for student use. Designed to promote higher-level learning and provide a bit of fun, the sheets invite students to use many kinds of skills in a variety of interesting activities. Of course, you may photocopy the sheets for distribution to your classes.

The answer key, beginning on page 74, provides solutions to many of the lessons' discussion questions and activities. No solutions are offered to open-ended questions.

The resources section, pages 81 through 84, lists books you can use for further study of each story's subject matter. Most are available in public libraries.

We hope you'll find this guide a useful supplement to *Many Voices*, and we'd like to hear from you if you have any suggestions or questions.

Anne Hutchinson

Jonathan Kruk

Objectives

Students should be able to 1) compare the religious beliefs of the Puritans with those of Anne Hutchinson and Native Americans and 2) analyze the cause-and-effect relationships between the British presence in New England and attacks by local tribes.

Background

Most students will name religious freedom as a reason the Puritans left England for America. They may not be aware, though, that whereas the Puritans wanted the freedom to establish a community run in accordance with the stringent rules of their church, they were not willing to extend such freedom to those with conflicting religious beliefs.

Discuss the rights and privileges of women in the new colony. Note that women were not allowed to vote or own land and that it was illegal for them to preach. Ask the students to speculate about what would have happened to a woman who violated the law against preaching—particularly if that woman espoused different religious beliefs.

Words to know: tribunal, heresy, sachem, pemmican, tinderbox, manitou, magistrate

Initiating activity

Have the students imagine they are Native Americans seeing Europeans for the first time. Beards were unknown to the native people, who believed the Europeans were animals pretending to be men. What else would seem strange to them? Students might role-play a discussion among a group of Mahican Indians, for instance, as they observe white settlers from a hidden vantage point.

Discussion questions

1. How did Anne Hutchinson's religious beliefs differ from those of the Puritans?
2. Why did Anne dismiss Captain Underhill's concerns about Governor Winthrop by saying, "He knows I am only preaching to women"?
3. What did the tribunal ask Anne to do to "save her soul"? What else might Anne have done to avoid banishment—or to avoid being called into court in the first place?
4. What was Director-General Kieft's main reason for welcoming new settlers? How did he aggravate the tension between white settlers and Native Americans?
5. What was Wampage's reason for attacking Anne Hutchinson's settlement? Was it Anne's fault? Do you think she would have blamed or forgiven him?

Follow-up activity

Write a diary entry for Susannah that describes the attack on the settlement. Include her thoughts on why the Wappinger people chose to attack.

Name _____

Directions: Use the chart below to compare and contrast the religious beliefs of Anne Hutchinson, the Native Americans, and the Puritans.

Anne Hutchinson	Native Americans	Puritans

The attack by the Wappinger people on Anne Hutchinson's little settlement had several causes. Analyze the direct and indirect causes of the attack, and fill in the graphic below.

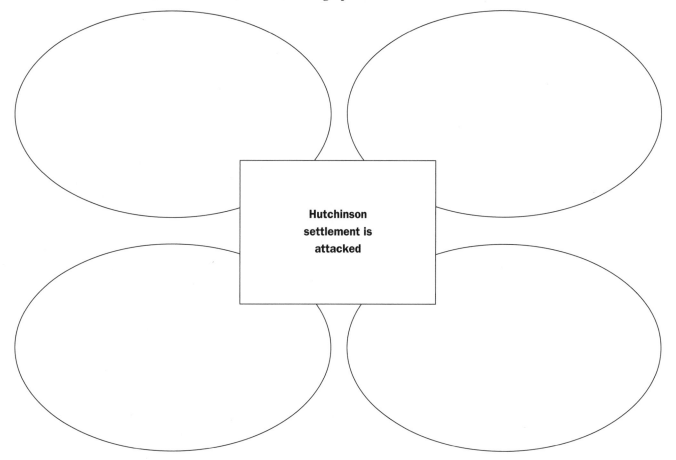

The Man Who Would Not Change His Name

Judith Kinter

Objectives

Students should be able to 1) identify when stubbornness is and is not a useful quality and 2) list sources of political unrest in England in the late 1600s.

Background

Review the historical context of this story: The Puritans—also called Roundheads and led by Oliver Cromwell—passed laws to limit the power of the king. Those loyal to the king were called Cavaliers. The two factions later became the Tories (Cavaliers), who represented the aristocracy and supported the divine right of kings, and the Whigs (Roundheads), who represented middle-class businessmen and felt Parliament should have power over the king.

Words to know: Roundhead, Cavalier

Initiating activity

Discuss the quality of stubbornness. When is it good to be stubborn about something? When is it undesirable? Put the graphic below on the board, and fill it in as you elicit responses from students.

Stubbornness

Good	Bad

Discussion questions

1. The story's author writes, "The air bristled with hostility." Have you ever witnessed such a situation? Does having two hostile political parties generally help or hurt a country?
2. In his life as a fugitive Caleb left many human casualties behind him. How did his stubbornness affect Caroline Potter, Caleb's cousin Weldon, the Puritans who helped him in Boston, and the McDaniels family?
3. Was Caleb himself a casualty of his own stubbornness? How would his life have been different if he had taken a new name when he arrived in Boston? What else could he have done to make sure the Cavaliers would not be able to identify him?
4. If the members of a political group were pursuing someone with whose principles you agreed, would you give that person shelter and protection? What factors would you have to consider before making that decision?

Follow-up activity

Have students find out how they got their first names. Group the various sources—for example, family name, named after a celebrity, parents just liked the name, and so on. Present the results of the survey on a poster-sized bar graph or bulletin-board display.

Student Activity Sheet • Many Voices • The Man Who Would Not Change His Name

Name_____

Directions: Write an acrostic poem, using the letters of your name. The words or phrases you choose should accurately represent you and your characteristics.

Example:

T	Terrific baseball player		S	Sensible
O	Often late getting up for school		M	Messy room
M	MTV fan		I	Insatiable chocolate-chip-cookie eater
			T	Tolerant of others' opinions
			H	Hoping to go to the college I choose

Write your poem in the space below.

Ticonderoga

Joseph Bruchac

Objectives

Students should be able to 1) find connections between the words *vengeance*, *guilt*, and *honor* and 2) evaluate the concept of "blood for blood."

Background

The conflict known as the French and Indian War of 1754–63 was the North American counterpart of the Seven Years' War between England and France. At its conclusion France lost Canada to Great Britain. Fort Ticonderoga, built in 1755 between Lakes George and Champlain in northeastern New York, was the site of an important battle in the war.

Words to know: sanctuary, kinsmen, dirk, clan, specter, ramparts, flotilla

Initiating activities

- Have the students work in small groups to brainstorm ideas about the words *vengeance*, *guilt*, and *honor*. Ask them to look for connections between the three words. Discuss as a whole group whether "blood for blood" is ever justifiable. What are some alternatives?
- Explain that one of the characters in this story is a ghost. Place this story in 1758, and remind students that people in those days were considerably more superstitious and often believed in ghosts and witches. (In 1692 in Salem, Massachusetts, for example, 20 people accused of witchcraft were executed.)

Discussion questions

1. How did Duncan Campbell get himself into a no-win situation when a stranger asked for sanctuary?
2. Do you think Duncan Campbell's guilt was making his mind play tricks on him? Why or why not?
3. Why did the troops of the Black Watch keep such a careful eye on Duncan Campbell as they journeyed up the river toward the French fort?
4. General Abercromby's decision to attack the fort head-on proved foolish as well as tragic. If General Howe had not been killed, what strategy do you think he would have used?
5. In your opinion, did Duncan Campbell get what he deserved for sheltering his cousin's murderer?

Follow-up activities

- On a map of New York, trace the route followed by Duncan Campbell's regiment up the Hudson River from New York City to Albany and then north across Lake George to the present town of Ticonderoga.
- The Mohawk tribe was part of the Iroquois League, an advanced confederation of North American Indian nations in the Hudson Valley area. Find out more about their leaders Cornplanter, Red Jacket, and Joseph Brant (Thayendanegea).

Student Activity Sheet • Many Voices • Ticonderoga

Name _____

Directions: At several points in this story Duncan Campbell could have made a different decision and changed the outcome of events.

Choose one of the following events and write it in box A below.
1. A stranger comes to Duncan Campbell's door asking for sanctuary.
2. Duncan's kinsmen tell him his cousin Donald has been murdered.
3. Donald's ghost tells Duncan that he has come to Ticonderoga.
4. General Abercromby orders the men to attack the fort head-on.

Write the consequences of the event (the decision Duncan made) in box B.

In box C, write an alternate decision that Duncan could have made.

In box D, summarize the probable outcome if Duncan had made that decision.

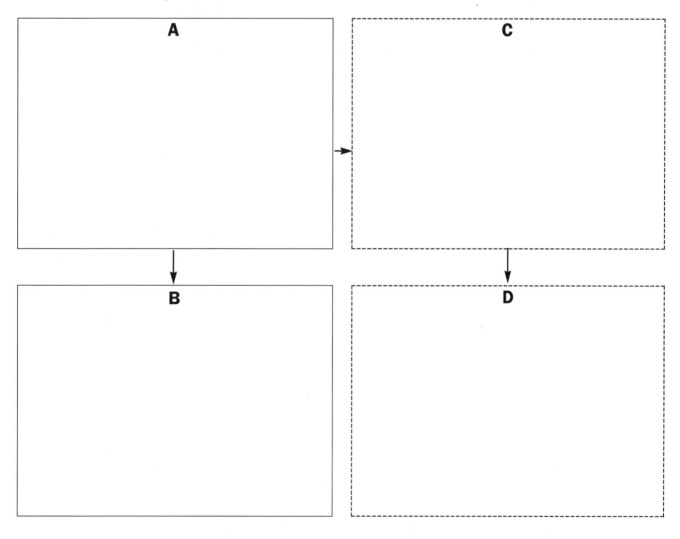

Lydia Darragh

Jack Briggs _____

Objectives

Students should be able to 1) explain the position pacifist Quakers found themselves in during the American Revolutionary War and 2) identify Lydia Darragh and evaluate her contribution as an American patriot.

Background

Discuss the establishment of the Pennsylvania Colony by William Penn, a Quaker who viewed his colony as a haven for persecuted religious groups. Discuss the Quaker religion, founded in 17th-century England by George Fox, who believed people could receive spiritual guidance by following their own "inward light" rather than being led by a clergyman. Also discuss the Quaker tenet of pacifism, which is important in this story.

Initiating activities

- Take a class vote on the following question: You are a Quaker during the American Revolution. You believe in the American cause, but your religion says you must not fight in wars. Will you help the American patriots win the war anyway?
- Discuss: During the Revolution one group of Quakers supported the cause of the patriots and believed in taking up arms for liberty. They were called Free Quakers. Besides serving in combat, what opportunities might have existed for Free Quakers to assist in the war effort?

Discussion questions

1. Why was General Howe in Philadelphia for the winter of 1777–78? What made him trust Lydia Darragh? What should he have known about Charles Darragh?
2. How was the Darragh family able to remain in their home when the British troops ordered them to leave? How was the patriots' cause helped by the British military's decision to let the Darraghs remain?
3. What do you think would have happened to Lydia if she had been caught listening in on the staff meeting?
4. Why do you suppose Lydia did not tell her husband about the information she had overheard? Why didn't she send the message through John?
5. In the question General Howe's aide asked Lydia, what key words allowed her to answer "no"? Do you think she would have admitted to being awake if he had phrased his question differently? Do you think he knew she was awake?
6. What might have happened if Lydia Darragh had heeded her husband's advice and stayed home?

Follow-up activity

On a city map of Philadelphia, find Germantown, Second Street, and Broad Street. Note that there is a historic Free Quaker Meeting House at Fifth and Arch streets. To the west of the city, locate Valley Forge (Whitemarsh).

Student Activity Sheet • Many Voices • Lydia Darragh

Name _____

Directions: Lydia Darragh's husband, William, created a secret code in which to send messages to General Washington. Below is a coded message that Lydia might have written. Break the code, and print the message in the spaces below.

U W T R T K U G   C V V C E M   D T K V K U J

_ _ _ _ _ _ _ _   _ _ _ _ _ _   _ _ _ _ _ _ _

O C T E J   C V   O K F P K I J V

_ _ _ _ _   _ _   _ _ _ _ _ _ _ _

Now create your own code, and write another short message Lydia Darragh might have sent at an earlier or later time. Print your coded message below, and write the solution on the back of your paper. Give your message to a partner to solve. No peeking!

Gone to War

Lucinda Flodin

Objectives

Students should be able to 1) evaluate the tragedy of war from the viewpoint of mothers on all sides (British, American, Native American) and 2) compare their own responsibilities and lifestyle with those of a frontier girl.

Background

Students often think of the American Revolution as being fought primarily in the Northeast, but from 1778–81 the major battles took place in the South, climaxing with Cornwallis's surrender at Yorktown, Virginia.

Watauga was a settlement founded by John Sevier in what is now East Tennessee. The settlers hoped to form a new state, to be called Franklin, but that never came to pass. In 1780 British troops persuaded a Cherokee chief, Dragging Canoe, to attack the Watauga settlement while most of its men were fighting at Kings Mountain. Fortunately the men returned home in time to prevent what might have been a massacre.

Words to know: retribution, muster, flintlock

Prereading or telling: Discuss the following questions with the whole group, or have students free-write for a few minutes and then share their responses: What are some things that go through your mind when you are home by yourself? What things do you worry about? What do you do if you get scared?

Discussion questions

1. The mother in this story says, "There's part of my heart breaking for all the women." Do you think other women have felt this way about war?
2. Do you find it ironic that Reverend Doak urges the men at the muster to march out and kill other men? Is that justifiable?
3. How was home life on the frontier different from life in Boston or Philadelphia? How do the 12-year-old character's chores and lifestyle compare with yours?
4. If Dragging Canoe had attacked the settlement, what would the character's responsibilities have been? What would be some possible outcomes?
5. Why do you think Ferguson called the mountain men "backwater men"?

Follow-up activities

- Explain that Native Americans were resentful of whites who took possession of the land the Indians had roamed for centuries. Discuss the European concept of private property and the view taken by Native Americans that the land was entrusted to all living creatures by the Creator. Have students postulate reasons for Native American alliances with the British. What did Native Americans hope to gain?
- Many enslaved African-Americans sided with the patriots during the Revolutionary War, then appealed for their freedom when the war ended. What arguments do you imagine they used to try to obtain freedom when the war ended?
- Create a journal entry written by Josiah, Mathew, or Benjamin on the way back home.

Student Activity Sheet • Many Voices • *Gone to War*

Name _____

Directions: An interior monologue records a character's thoughts in a given situation. For example, an interior monologue for someone running in a marathon might include thoughts such as *I can do it. I know I can finish.* Write an interior monologue for the narrator of "Gone to War" on the night she is left alone while her mother helps to deliver a baby. Use the "thought balloons" below to organize your thoughts before you begin to write.

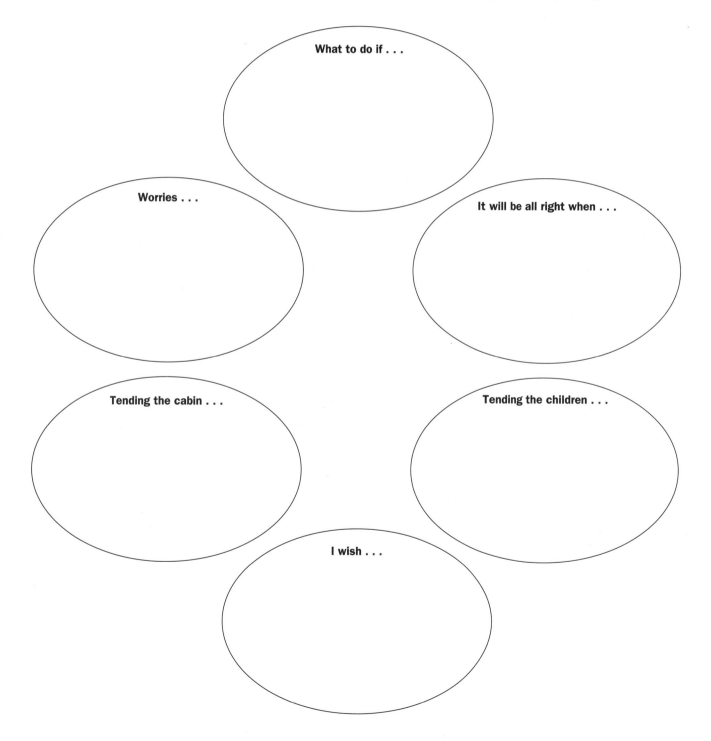

What to do if . . .

Worries . . .

It will be all right when . . .

Tending the cabin . . .

Tending the children . . .

I wish . . .

Sacagawea's Story

Michael Carney

Objectives

Students should be able to 1) define manifest destiny, 2) identify Lewis and Clark and Sacagawea, and 3) evaluate the treatment of women in 1800.

Background

Discuss the Louisiana Purchase and the ideology of manifest destiny. Be sure students understand that Lewis and Clark were sent by President Thomas Jefferson to explore the land acquired in the Louisiana Purchase.

Initiating activities

- Speculate on why Americans kept moving farther west and why it was necessary to explore new territories before opening them to settlement. Discuss how the westward movement affected Native American populations, and point out that although their tribes were continually displaced, Native Americans were often friendly and helpful to whites. This is the story of a particularly brave Shoshone woman, Sacagawea, who was instrumental to the Lewis and Clark expedition.
- On a U.S. map, identify the general area they explored.

Discussion questions

1. Why did the expedition leaders need to see the Shoshones? If Sacagawea hadn't been with them, how might they have tried to communicate? Would they have succeeded in obtaining what they wanted from the Shoshones?
2. The members of the expedition "didn't see a single person all summer long." Is there anywhere you could go today to experience such solitude?
3. How did the tribal life Sacagawea described to the narrator differ from the lives that would be led by the settlers who would soon come west?
4. What evidence does the story give that Native American women were not treated as equals by men of their own tribe or by white men?
5. How do you think the Lewis and Clark expedition would have been different without Sacagawea's help?
6. Was Clark surprised that Sacagawea did not stay with her Shoshone family? Why do you think she made the decision she did?

Follow-up activities

- Discuss the effects of the Lewis and Clark expedition on American history.
- Imagine an incident that might have occurred during the expedition but was not included in the story. Tell your story to the class, from Sacagawea's viewpoint.
- Use your library to learn about Zebulon Pike, another explorer who was in the West at around the same time as Lewis and Clark.

Teller's tip

Brainstorm a list of problems likely to occur while traversing many miles of wilderness.

Name _____

Directions: Many U.S. states' names have their origins in the languages of various Native American tribes. Choose a state from the box that matches its Native American origin most closely. Then unscramble the circled letters to reveal the name of a famous Native American.

Alaska	Minnesota	Kentucky	Alabama
Mississippi	Wyoming	Michigan	Idaho
Massachusetts			

Native American words	Meaning	U.S. state name
me si pi	"big river"	1. __ __Ⓞ__ __ __ __ __ __ __ __
mish e gen	"big water"	2. __ __ __ __ Ⓞ __ __
wachusett	"great hill"	3. __Ⓞ__ __ __ __ __ __ __ __ __ __ __
minne sota	"water the color of the sky"	4. __ __ __ Ⓞ __ __ __ __
ken tah teh	"meadow land"	5. __ __ __ __ Ⓞ __ __
alaeksu	"great land"	6. __ __Ⓞ__ __ __ __
maughwauwame	"on the great plain"	7. Ⓞ__ __ __ __ __ __ __
ee dah how	"sun on the mountain"	8. __ __Ⓞ__ __
alba amo	"people who clear land"	9. Ⓞ__ __ __ __ __ __ __

Famous Native American: __ __ __ __ __ __ __ __ __

A Love Story

Ruth Stotter

Objectives

Students should be able to 1) locate the Presidio on a modern map, 2) examine various kinds of love, and 3) evaluate the wisdom of basing one's life decisions on "true love."

Background

Review the history of Southern California, claimed for Spain in 1542 but ceded in 1848 to the United States. On a map, locate San Francisco and the Presidio. Also find Sitka, Alaska, and point out how close Russia is to the Alaskan border. Remind students that Alaska was controlled by Russia until the United States purchased it in 1867.

Words to know: commandant, scurvy, czar

Initiating activity

As a class, brainstorm about the word *love*. You might use a web like this one:

What is it? How do you know you're in love?

Love

What kinds are there? What problems can being in love cause?

Discussion questions

1. What did Concha see from the hillside outside her home? What would she see today from the same location?
2. What kinds of love are evident in this story?
3. Why was Concha's brother unable to help Rezanoff? How did Rezanoff deal with the refusal of help? Do you think it was a scheme on his part?
4. Do you think Concha was right to "follow her heart"? Do you think Rezanoff intended to come back and marry her? Should she have tried to forget him?
5. Do you think it was unfair of Concha's father not to show her the letter he received from Alexander Baranov? Do you think Concha's life would have been any different if he had shown it to her?

Follow-up activity

On small slips of paper, write phrases that Rezanoff might have used when he put into port in San Francisco. (Examples: "We have otter pelts to trade." "Our people in Alaska are hungry.") Distribute these to students, and explain that they must communicate their messages (to a small group or the whole class) without using any words.

Teller's tip

Ask each student to prepare a short monologue from one character's point of view. Characters could include Concha, members of her family, Rezanoff, another nun in Benicia, or a child at the school. As the students re-create a character's life, they should interweave their perceptions of Concepción so the stories tie together.

Student Activity Sheet • Many Voices • *A Love Story*

Name _____

Directions: You are Concepción Arguello. You are 18 years old, and two years ago Rezanoff, the man who asked you to be his bride, began a long journey to ask the czar's permission to go ahead with the wedding. Recently, though, you've heard that a married man named Rezanoff lives at Fort Ross, north of your home in Yerba Buena. You decide to write a letter to the commandant at the fort in an attempt to find out what has happened to your husband-to-be.

The Presidio
Yerba Buena
(date) 18_____

Dear Commandant,

Sincerely,

Concepción Arguello

Tsali: Cherokee Hero
Of the Smoky Mountains

Duncan Sings-Alone _____

Objectives

Students should be able to 1) locate the lands belonging to the Eastern Cherokee before their removal to Oklahoma, 2) consider the perspectives of both whites and Cherokees, and 3) identify Tsali and explain why he is a hero to his people.

Background

Using a U.S. map, show students the lands originally belonging to the Eastern Cherokee nation, and trace the trails followed during the forced removal.

Words to know: syllabary, populist, legislative fiat, retribution, martyr

Initiating activities

• Ask how many students in the class have moved from a different state. As you elicit responses, have the students locate their old homes on the map and estimate how many miles they traveled in the move. Now ask everyone to react to the idea of being forced by the government to make such a move—and of walking that distance with no protection from the winter cold except a blanket.

• Have students speculate on reasons why one person wants another's land. What are some pieces of land in their community that might be considered valuable? Why? Ask students to brainstorm some alternatives to forcing people to leave their homes.

Discussion questions

1. What did you learn about Cherokee culture? Were you surprised?
2. How did the Congress vote on the removal of the Cherokees? Who reversed its decision? Who decided to ignore the reversal? Would this be allowed to happen today?
3. Describe the removal and what was left behind.
4. What was the biggest mistake the young Georgia militiaman made?
5. Why did General Scott want Tsali and his sons to be shot by their own people? Did his plan work?

Follow-up activities

• Write a persuasive letter to your elected representatives in the Congress, requesting that a day in early spring be legally designated to honor Native Americans. Describe some of the activities that might take place on such a day.

• Find out more about the life of Sequoya, who developed the syllabary that led to the publication of newspapers and books in the Cherokee language. Make a poster of the syllabary. Teach your classmates some Cherokee words.

Teller's tip

The children could look for pictures of Indian tribes and note what is different about their clothing and adornments. It is important to look at pictures of both modern and historical Indians. Many Americans believe that Indians are an extinct species or that Indians live primitive lifestyles.

Student Activity Sheet • Many Voices • Tsali: Cherokee Hero of the Smoky Mountains

Name _____

Directions: Design a commemorative coin honoring Tsali and his sons.

Tom Stowe

Paul Leone _____

Objectives

Students should be able to 1) identify the Underground Railroad, 2) examine slavery from the perspective of both slaves and their masters, and 3) evaluate the character of those who helped slaves to escape.

Background

Explain what the Underground Railroad was and when it operated. Have students trace the Ohio River, which separated free and slave states.

Words to know: steamship, bounty hunter

Initiating activities

- Ask students to discuss the idea that one person could own another. How would being a slave compare to being in prison? If you were a slave, what might you try to do about your situation?
- Explain that by 1850 steamships traveled on the nation's rivers. Have students locate Vicksburg, Mississippi, and ask them how they would get from there to Memphis; Louisville; Cincinnati; and Morgantown, West Virginia.

Discussion questions

1. How did Tom get his last name? Was Henry Stowe proud of Tom in the way your parents are proud of you? Why did he trust Tom to stay alone in Morgantown?
2. How do you imagine Tom felt as he rode the steamship and tended the horses?
3. What was Tom's main reason for refusing to consider Mr. Burgess's suggestion that freedom was just across the river? Did Tom trust Mr. Burgess?
4. What evidence is there that Henry Stowe was responsible for Tom's decision to run away? Was Henry aware there might be a problem? Do you think he felt guilty?
5. If Tom were able to tell you how he felt as he slept in the secret room at the farmhouse, what do you think he would say?
6. Where did Tom end up? What do you imagine happened after he arrived there?

Follow-up activities

- Set up the classroom with the various settings and scenes in the story, assigning a few students to each "station." Have the students who are "in Vicksburg" stage a scene with Tom, Lucy, and their child and a later scene with Lucy, Henry Stowe, and Tom. In other parts of the room, add scenes on the steamship, in Mr. Burgess's store, in the Pennsylvania woods, along the road, at the farmhouse, at Mr. Petit's house, and finally on the boat Tom takes to Canada. Encourage the students to improvise, adding dialogue, asides by various characters, and so forth. Give the students time to practice, and then put all the scenes together in a retelling of the story.
- Summarize the story from the viewpoint of Henry Stowe, Mr. Burgess, or Tom's little boy. Keep in mind that these characters won't know the whole story.

Student Activity Sheet • Many Voices • Tom Stowe

Name _____

Directions: "Will I remain a slave, Henry Stowe's property? Or should I make a break for freedom, as Mr. Burgess suggested?" In making this decision, Tom had to weigh the pros and cons of slavery versus an attempt at freedom. Work with a small group to list some reasons for staying and some reasons for running away.

Reasons for staying	Reasons for running away

Do you think Tom made the best decision?

If you were Tom, which reason would be the most important factor? Why?

Westward Migration: Nancy Robbins's Story

Katherine Lesperance

Objectives

Students should be able to 1) explain the significance of the Oregon Trail, 2) list reasons people went west, and 3) enumerate hardships faced by those migrating west.

Background

The treaty of 1846 settled the Oregon boundary dispute with Great Britain, and the war with Mexico gave California and New Mexico to the United States two years later. The West was open for settlement.

Words to know: cholera, naturalist

Initiating activities

- After pointing out the Oregon Trail on a map, have students divide into westward-bound "families" of four or five and answer the following questions: Why do we want to go to Oregon? What hardships might there be on the trail? What kinds of things will we need to take with us?
- A week or so before working with this story, and others about the westward movement, send a note home to parents, asking for photocopies of old letters, diaries, photos, etc., related to pioneers in the students' families who moved west. Even better, invite grand-parents or parents into the classroom to relate stories of their families' move west.

Discussion questions

1. What did Nancy Robbins dream of as she thought about moving to Oregon?
2. What kind of attitude did Nancy Robbins have, and how did that help others who were part of the wagon train? Was Nancy a good "team player"?
3. Nathaniel asked the children what new thing they discovered each day. Tell about something new you've discovered lately.
4. Compare Mrs. McGibney's and Mr. Steed's feelings about Indians.
5. Was Nathaniel being unfeeling when he urged Nancy to be strong after Mahala's death? How do you think your mother would have acted in Nancy's place?
6. How did the Robbins family's dreams about the journey to Oregon compare with actual events? What kept Nancy going in spite of all her troubles?

Follow-up activities

- Have students tell a story like Nathaniel might have told around the campfire about the prosperity that awaited the family in Oregon.
- Discuss how the stereotypical image of circled wagons and attacking Indians often shown in Westerns compares with Nancy Robbins's depiction in this story.

Teller's tip

Try a wagon-train exercise: Give the students an imaginary wagon with a weight limit of 5,000 pounds. Then give them a huge list of possible things to pack. Let them select what they would bring, and have them explain each item's relative importance.

Student Activity Sheet • Many Voices • *Westward Migration: Nancy Robbins's Story*

Name _____

Directions: Add another episode to the story—one year after the family settles in Oregon City. Use the framework below to jot down notes for your story. Then tell it aloud to your classmates.

At last, here we are in _____ . Nathaniel was mostly

right about Oregon, but _____

_____ .

The last weeks on the trail were _____ .

I still can't forget the time _____

_____ .

And only a few days later, _____

_____ .

We got through it all by _____ ,

and now _____ . I have a brand-new

_____ , and I'm looking forward to

_____ .

I often think of Mahala, but _____

_____

_____ .

Willie the Handcart Boy

John L. Beach

Objectives

Students should be able to 1) relate how the Mormons' religious faith helped them face impossible odds, 2) locate Salt Lake City, and 3) identify Brigham Young.

Background

"Mormon" is the name commonly used to refer to a member of the Church of Jesus Christ of Latter-day Saints, organized by Joseph Smith in 1831 in New York. The hostility of the church's neighbors caused the Mormons to keep moving west. In Illinois, Smith and his brother were murdered by a mob. Brigham Young led the Mormons to Utah, where they founded Salt Lake City and established a communal economy.

Words to know: Zion, handcart

Initiating activities

- Mormons believe in the importance of revelation. After a huge swarm of crickets invaded their first crops in Utah, the Mormons took it as a sign from heaven when a flock of seagulls flew in behind the crickets and devoured them. Have the students discuss how signs of various kinds can help us live our lives.
- Assignment: It is 1856. Your family is very poor, but because of your religious faith it is of utmost importance to get to a place in Utah known as Zion. You will have to push and pull your belongings from Florence, Nebraska, to the Great Salt Lake valley in a large handcart. Everyone in the family will need to work as hard as possible for several months. What thoughts race through your mind the night before your departure?

Discussion questions

1. At the beginning of the story, how do you know the handcart trip has been hard?
2. Describe Mr. and Mrs. Blair's reactions to Helen's death. Formulate some possible reasons for their feelings. Is this how your parents would react?
3. How does Captain Martin's request for Willie's help affect Willie? Compare the captain's trust in Willie with a similar trust an adult has placed in you.
4. Was it a good idea for Mr. Blair to get wet and cold helping others to ford the river? How do you think the others would have treated him if he had not helped?
5. Why do you think Captain Martin kept the group moving in spite of the snowstorm? If they had stopped sooner, what could they have used for shelter?
6. What made it possible for the Mormons in this story to keep going?
7. What do you think Willie and Nancy learned from this journey? How do you think they had changed by the time they arrived in Utah?

Follow-up activities

- Tell a story about a time you had to call on inner strength to get through an experience that was frightening or dangerous. How did you feel afterward?
- Write a letter Mrs. Madison or Mrs. Blair might have sent to relatives back home.

Student Activity Sheet • Many Voices • Willie the Handcart Boy

Name _____

Directions: When authors write fictional stories based on fact, some of the information they include is true and some they create in order to make their stories interesting. Opinions are neither fiction nor fact but matters of belief that are implied by the author or inferred by the reader.

Analyze each statement below. Decide whether it is factual, fictional, or an opinion. Mark it with F, A, or O.

Factual = F   **Fictional = A**   **Opinion = O**

_____ 1. Captain Edward Martin operated a handcart company in the 1800s.

_____ 2. Willie Madison was a British immigrant who was a Mormon.

_____ 3. The Mormons' strong faith helped them endure many hardships.

_____ 4. Nancy Madison pulled the family's handcart by herself while Willie helped the Blairs.

_____ 5. God led the Mormons to the Great Salt Lake valley.

_____ 6. Mrs. Blair sold vegetables to make a living in Utah.

_____ 7. Helen Blair died of exposure.

_____ 8. Pioneers helped one another out more than people do today.

_____ 9. Willie often thought of Helen when he looked at the mountains.

_____ 10. In 1856 many Mormons perished when their handcart party was caught in a blizzard.

Write your own statement of each kind below.

Factual:

Fictional:

Opinion:

Pioneering Spirit: The Story of Julia Archibald Holmes

John Stansfield

Objectives

Students should be able to 1) locate Pikes Peak, 2) differentiate between espousing beliefs and acting on them, 3) evaluate the character attributes of Julia Archibald Holmes, and 4) consider westward migration from a Native American viewpoint.

Background

Have one student find Pikes Peak, Colorado, while another locates Boston. Estimate the distance between the two, and speculate on transportation modes used by travelers from Boston to Colorado in 1858. The importance of the railroads should be emphasized: how they changed accessibility to the prairie, brought cheap labor in the form of immigrants, and further compromised the lifestyles of Native Americans.

Words to know: abolitionist, free state, bloomer, suffrage, reform

Initiating activity

Use the framework below to discuss voting rights.

Who had the right to vote in colonial times?   Who has it now?

The right to vote

Why is voting so important?   How would things be different today if only women could vote?

Discussion questions

1. The letters Julia wrote to her family and to a women's magazine were important sources for this story. If you went on a long trip today, you might call home or even send electronic mail from your laptop computer. How do Julia's communication methods and today's high-tech methods compare from the standpoint of preserving history? What ways to record history are available to us that were not available in 1858? Which methods are more reliable? More interesting?
2. Analyze the values Julia learned from her parents. Are they good values for living in today's world? How did the Archibalds act on their beliefs?
3. What does Julia's mode of dress indicate about her character? How do you think she would dress today if she were a high-school or middle-school student?
4. What organizations would Julia be likely to join if she were alive today?
5. Why do you think Julia enjoyed her journey more than most of her companions?
6. Do you think Julia was the first woman who ever climbed Pikes Peak?

Follow-up activities

- Julia took a volume of Emerson's writings with her on the climb up Pikes Peak. Read some of Emerson's work, and identify some probable reasons why Julia enjoyed it.
- Define *pioneer* as it applies to this story as well as to scientific research, the arts, human rights, and technology. Identify some areas explored by modern pioneers.

Name _____

Directions: Imagine that you are a reporter for a Kansas newspaper. When Julia returns to Lawrence, Kansas, to visit her family, you're lucky enough to get an exclusive interview with her. Write at least five key questions you will ask her. Your questions should be open-ended—in other words, they should call for more than a simple "yes" or "no" answer. (If you like, use the back of your paper to write more questions.) Then trade papers with another student. Write Julia's answers to the questions.

1. Question: _____

   Answer: _____

   _____

2. Question: _____

   Answer: _____

   _____

3. Question: _____

   Answer: _____

   _____

4. Question: _____

   Answer: _____

   _____

5. Question: _____

   Answer: _____

   _____

Why Lincoln Grew a Beard

Lucille Breneman

Objectives

Students should be able to 1) use facts, quotations, and this story about Lincoln to develop an understanding of the sort of person he was, 2) compare presidential privacy and the campaign and voting practices of 1860 with those of the present day, and 3) list technological advances not available in 1860.

Background

Elicit information about Abraham Lincoln from students, and fill in what they may not know. Lincoln was the 16th U.S. president. He was born in a log cabin, was mostly self-educated, and became a lawyer. He served in the Congress, then joined the then-new Republican party and engaged in a series of seven debates with Stephen Douglas. In 1860 he was elected president with a minority of the popular vote. Before his inauguration seven states seceded from the union, and the Civil War soon began. In 1863 he signed the Emancipation Proclamation and delivered the Gettysburg Address. Lincoln saw the end of the war but was assassinated by John Wilkes Booth on April 14, 1865.

Initiating activity

Discuss or write about the following quotes by Abraham Lincoln: "Die when I may, I want it said of me by those who knew me best, that I always plucked a thistle and planted a flower where I thought a flower would grow." "There is a certain kind of success that is due to selfishness." "An ant's life is as sweet to it as ours is to us."

Discussion questions

1. Why did Grace Bedell think that ladies who liked Lincoln's whiskers would tell their husbands to vote for him? Would such ladies vote for him themselves?
2. To what extent do you think people base their votes on a candidate's appearance?
3. How do you think the volume of mail Abraham Lincoln received compares with that received at the White House today? Who do you think answers most of the letters sent to the president today?
4. Does the argument between John Nicolay and John Hay remind you of any interactions between politicians that you have seen on television?
5. Why didn't Grace already know that Lincoln had grown whiskers before she saw him in person? How much has the privacy of politicians, especially that of the president, changed since Lincoln's time?
6. What made Lincoln so popular with some groups yet so unpopular with others? Do "good" presidents often have administrations filled with turmoil?
7. How does Lincoln's campaign for president compare with presidential campaigns in recent years? What are some tactics politicians use to try to get elected?

Follow-up activity

Write a letter to the president, stating your views on how to improve our country.

Student Activity Sheet • Many Voices • *Why Lincoln Grew a Beard*

Name _____

Directions: Look at each entry below. Decide whether the item, trend, or person existed in the United States in 1860. Write **Y** next to those you think did exist. Write **N** next to those that did not.

_____ 1. steamboats

_____ 2. kaleidoscopes

_____ 3. electric lamps

_____ 4. Webster's dictionary

_____ 5. matches

_____ 6. newspapers

_____ 7. federal income tax

_____ 8. *Frankenstein*
(a novel by Mary Shelley)

_____ 9. airplanes

_____ 10. health insurance

_____ 11. sewing machines

_____ 12. railroads

_____ 13. calculators

_____ 14. cellophane

_____ 15. antibiotics

_____ 16. Braille

_____ 17. theaters

_____ 18. *The Adventures of Huckleberry Finn*
(a novel by Mark Twain)

_____ 19. nuclear reactors

_____ 20. magazines

_____ 21. teddy bears

_____ 22. radios

_____ 23. *Walden*
(a book by Henry David Thoreau)

_____ 24. the YMCA

_____ 25. drivers' licenses

_____ 26. gasoline engines

_____ 27. Social Security

_____ 28. *The Tale of Peter Rabbit*
(a children's book by Beatrix Potter)

_____ 29. the telegraph

_____ 30. the Erie Canal

_____ 31. *David Copperfield*
(a novel by Charles Dickens)

_____ 32. stereos

_____ 33. microphones

_____ 34. atomic bombs

_____ 35. personal computers

A Cold Night

R. Craig Roney

Objectives

Students should be able to 1) discuss the concept of respect for the dead, 2) define *dehumanization* and explain its relationship to war, and 3) write their own ghost stories—including some historical facts—set in the Civil War era.

Background

The Civil War is often called the bloodiest conflict in U.S. history. Discuss why so many died such agonizing deaths in this war. (For example, there was much hand-to-hand combat, and the weaponry was advanced enough to inflict horrific wounds, yet physicians did not have the knowledge, medicine, and skills needed to save lives.)

Words to know: picket, breastwork

Initiating activity

Locate Nashville, the Stones River, and Murfreesboro on a map of Tennessee. Show students where the Confederate and Union troops were located. To give students an idea of the relative sizes of the armies—and after reading, of the huge number of casualties— compare the number of soldiers to the number of students in your school or the population of your community. (For example, if your school has 500 students, the 45,000-member Union force was 90 times as big.)

Discussion questions

1. What were Rosecrans' and Bragg's immediate and long-term objectives?
2. What factors contributed to a Union victory? What might have changed the outcome?
3. How does the description of the sergeant foreshadow the outcome of this story?
4. Why do you think the surgeon acted as he did? Was he acting out of scientific inquiry or for some other reason? How do you suppose the other soldiers reacted?
5. What thoughts do you imagine went through the minds of the soldiers on both sides on the silent, cold night the story describes?
6. Could this story be true? Do you think it is? How could you find out if it's possible?

Follow-up activities

- Writing idea: In what ways is it customary in our culture and in others to show respect for the dead?
- On the board, use a Venn diagram to compare the soldiers on both sides of the battlefield. Have students use the same diagram individually to compare the surgeon and Bierce's friend.
- Discuss dehumanization as a result of war. Students who have read Erich Maria Remarque's novel *All Quiet on the Western Front* (Little, Brown, 1975) or watched the movie might compare its main character with the soldiers depicted in this story. Students should identify other sources of dehumanization in their world.

Student Activity Sheet • Many Voices • A Cold Night

Name _____

Directions: Your assignment is to write a ghost story set during the Civil War. Your story, like "A Cold Night," should include some factual information to add authenticity. Use the planning chart below before you begin to write.

Setting: Choose the scene of an actual battle, the home town of a war hero, the Confederate or Union capital, or some other Civil War–related setting. _____

_____

_____

What took place in this setting that you might include in your story? _____

_____

Real character(s): Choose at least one character who really lived and was present in this setting. _____

_____

Main character: This character should be fictional. _____

_____

Minor characters: These should be fictional. _____

_____

Conflict: What event will cause the tension and action in your story? _____

_____

_____

Ghostly element: What element of your story will give your readers or listeners "the creeps"?

_____

Details: What else will you put in your story to identify it with the Civil War era? You might mention who was president, for example, or refer to modes of transportation or a recently opened territory to the west.

_____

_____

_____

_____

The Story of Wilmer McLean

Mike T. Mullen

Objectives

Students should be able to 1) summarize the actual story of McLean, 2) analyze the effects of war on civilians, and 3) recognize the concepts of coincidence, irony, and intuition.

Background

When South Carolina became the first state to secede from the Union, it claimed Fort Sumter, but President James Buchanan refused to give up any federal forts in the South. Fort Sumter was besieged by the Confederates and finally surrendered to General Pierre Beauregard. After this action most Southerners thought that if war ensued, it would be a short conflict that the South would easily win. This story exemplifies one man's wish simply to keep his family safe. It includes examples of coincidence, intuition, and irony.

Words to know: states' rights

Initiating activity

To give students another perspective on how the war affected noncombatants, read some selections from Mary Boykin Chesnut's *A Diary From Dixie* (Harvard University Press, 1980). This personal account of how the war affected Southerners was often quoted in the PBS series *The Civil War.*

Discussion questions

1. How do you think citizens would react today if one state seceded from the United States and then attacked a military base within U.S. borders? What action do you think the federal government would take?

2. How does Wilmer's intuition help him on the morning of the first Battle of Bull Run? Have you ever had a similar feeling that something "just wasn't right"? Did your feeling prove to be true?

3. What is Wilmer's main concern during the battle and all through the war?

4. Would people ever gather to watch a battle today? Why or why not? In what other ways are we spectators of war? What sports events, television programs, and activities do people watch that involve danger and possible death for others? Why do you think people are attracted to such things?

5. Would Wilmer agree with the author that the Civil War was a great American tragedy? Support your answer.

6. Did you guess that the brick house mentioned at the end of the story would be Wilmer's? What makes this story so remarkable?

7. Did Wilmer agree with either side? Do you think he cared who won the war?

Follow-up activity

Role-play Lee's surrender to Grant. Students might include a scene in which one of Lee's aides makes arrangements to use the McLean home. Some students should take the roles of townspeople, who have varying reactions to the surrender. Others can play the roles of Wilmer, his wife, and his children.

Name _____

Directions: Write a diamanté, a diamond-shaped poem that follows the formula below and shows a strong contrast between its first and last lines. The body of the poem should build gradually toward the conclusion. The subject of the poem should be related to "The Story of Wilmer McLean." (One suggestion for the first and last lines: War . . . Peace.)

Formula	Example
1. One word: the subject of the poem	Heat
2. Two adjectives describing the subject in line 1	Sticky, oppressive
3. Three participles (*-ed* or *-ing* words)	Blazed, seared, unrelenting
4. Four words that relate to the subject in line 1	Sunburned beach, radios loud
5. Three participles leading toward line 7	Thundering, darkening, clouding
6. Two adjectives leading toward line 7	Rainy, gray
7. One word, the opposite of the subject in line 1	Cold

_____

_____   _____

_____   _____   _____

_____   _____   _____   _____

_____   _____   _____

_____   _____

_____

The Cardiff Giant

Martha Hamilton and Mitch Weiss

Objective

Students should be able to recognize possible hoaxes as well as misleading advertisements for products whose value is doubtful.

Background

Define and discuss free enterprise and some ways that the pursuit of wealth in a free-enterprise system can mislead consumers.

Words to know: petrified, geologist, barker, paleontologist

Initiating activity

Have the students bring in examples of suspected hoaxes in magazine and newspaper advertising. Some sure-to-finds are miracle weight-loss pills, potions to cure baldness, and "millionaires' secrets." Junk mail—especially the kind that makes it look as though the recipient has already won a fabulous prize—is another good source. Evaluate the examples for truth in advertising. Take votes: Who would have bought the product? Who wouldn't now? Which hoax is the worst?

Discussion questions

1. How wide is the back of your hand? How many times as big was the Cardiff Giant's hand?
2. Why were the residents of Cardiff happy to have so many people visit the giant? What kinds of businesses are successful in tourist areas?
3. ". . . Everybody wanted to chip just a little piece of stone from the giant man." Think of a business you could have opened in Cardiff.
4. Several theories attempted to explain where the giant man had come from. Which made the most sense? Think of another possible explanation.
5. Stub had a hard time moving the stone giant. How could he do it easily today?
6. Do you think Barnum's defense that he was "exhibiting a hoax of a hoax" was valid?
7. Does it surprise you that the Cardiff Giant became even more popular after people discovered it was definitely a fake? Should Stub have been prosecuted for taking people's money on false pretenses, or does the concept of "caveat emptor" protect him?

Follow-up activities

- Some other scams to discuss are roadside attractions, sideshows at fairs, and the stories often found in tabloids.
- Have small groups formulate some rules to help people avoid being taken in by misleading claims. Combine all the groups' rules, and make sure everyone has a copy to keep and a copy to share with someone who is not in your class.
- Have two students briefly research Oliver Wendell Holmes and Ralph Waldo Emerson and report to the class.
- Role-play the two barkers who tried to persuade people to see "their" giant.

Student Activity Sheet • *Many Voices* • *The Cardiff Giant*

Name _____

Directions: Create your own hoax. Use tabloids, magazines, newspapers, and television commercials for inspiration. You may present your hoax in any way you wish. Some suggestions follow:

- Tape it as a radio news announcement.
- Videotape it as a television infomercial.
- "Bark" about it at an imaginary carnival.
- Report it on an investigative-journalism program.
- Talk about it on a talk show.
- Paste it on the front of a popular tabloid.

On the balloon map below, let your thoughts flow freely as you plan your scam.

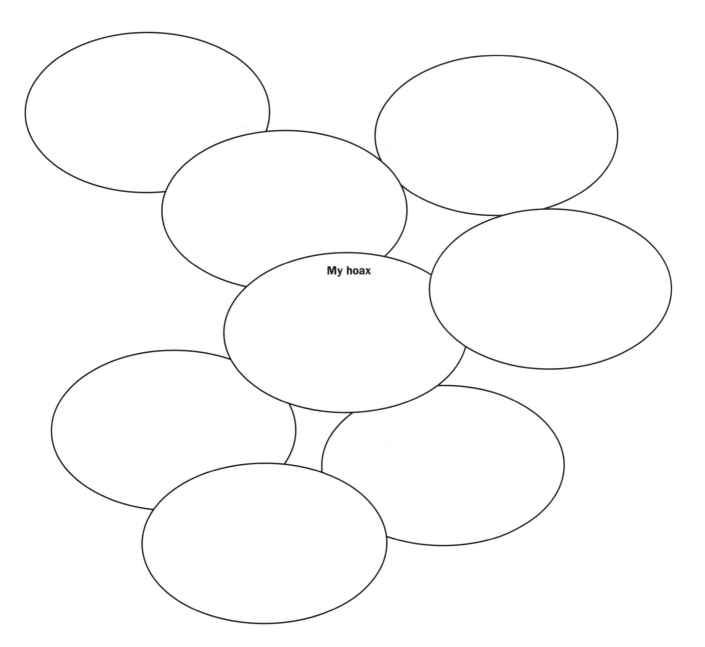

My hoax

Wild Bill Hickok in Springfield

Richard Alan Young and Judy Dockrey Young

Objective

Students should be able to name important elements of a town and identify at least one hero or villain of the Old West.

Background

Wild Bill Hickok was noted for his courage and particularly for his skill with a gun. As the cattle business grew in the West, small towns were often without a marshal or any form of law enforcement, so it was important that people be able to defend themselves. Hickok was shot while playing poker in Deadwood, South Dakota. The hand he held—a pair of eights and a pair of aces—is still called the "dead man's hand."

Tellers' tip

You may want to surround the story with facts about the era. Feel free to add descriptive words and to personalize and localize the story by referring to nearby geographic features or previously studied aspects of the American West.

Initiating activity

Discuss stereotypes of Western heroes students may have encountered in such movies as *Shane, High Noon,* and *Pale Rider.* Use a diagram like the one below to list some traits of a stereotypical Western hero. Extensions can be used for examples of traits.

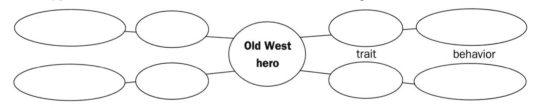

Discussion questions

1. Did Tutt really want Hickok's watch, or was something else at stake?
2. How did Tutt "dig his own grave"? What would have happened if he hadn't fired first? Did he make a wise decision?
3. How had Springfield changed between 1865 and 1873?
4. What can you infer about 1873 Springfield from the size of its jail?
5. Why did Wild Bill call John Stokes "Uncle"?
6. How does Stokes' way of dealing with Wild Bill compare with what would probably happen to you if the police caught you shooting out streetlights?

Follow-up activity

As Americans moved west, towns sprang up along the way. As a class, choose a location and name for a new town. Then make and prioritize a list of what the town will need in order to be a safe, prosperous home for its new residents. Students can take on the roles of the settlers and hold a "town meeting." Encourage them to try to represent the different viewpoints that would have been likely among a diverse group.

Student Activity Sheet • Many Voices • *Wild Bill Hickok in Springfield*

Name _____

Directions: Choose a famous Old West figure from the list below. Research your choice. Then draw a portrait and write a brief biography beneath it. If the person you choose is an outlaw, you might prefer to do this assignment as a wanted poster. Display your finished assignments on a wall designated as an Old West portrait gallery.

Buffalo Bill Cody	Chief Red Cloud	Annie Oakley	Geronimo
Calamity Jane	Elfego Baca	Jesse James	Isom Dart
Jim Bridger	Kit Carson	Sam Bass	Wyatt Earp
Bat Masterson	John Wesley Harding		

_____

_____

_____

Adapted from an idea by the authors, Richard Alan Young and Judy Dockrey Young

Inspector Walsh and Sitting Bull

Marie Anne McLean

Objective

Students should understand that negotiation is preferable to revolution and violence.

Background

Elicit basic information about Canada from students. Fill in with these facts (a map will be helpful): Canada has 10 provinces and two territories. Its capital is Ottawa. Both English and French are official languages of Canada. About 350,000 Native Canadians live in Canada. Most of its remaining 27 million citizens are of French or British origin. Most Canadians live along the southern edge of Canada, within 100 miles of the U.S. border.

Initiating activities

- In the southwest corner of Saskatchewan, locate Cypress Hills Provincial Park and Fort Walsh National Historic Park. Maple Creek is just to the northeast. Remind students that at the time of the story, this area of Canada was a wilderness.
- Ask a student scribe to jot notes on the board as you discuss with students the various ways to solve disputes between individuals, political parties, and nations.

Discussion questions

1. What did the North-West Mounted Police have in common with the United States Cavalry? What were some differences—and why were those differences important to the Sioux who had fled to Canada?
2. What might Sitting Bull have said to other members of his tribe when discussing Walsh?
3. Is it likely that officials in Ottawa really understood what Walsh had accomplished with the Sioux and why his accomplishments were important?
4. How do you imagine the constable's tone of voice as he responded to the cavalry officer's question at the end of the story? How do you imagine the expression on the cavalry officer's face when he heard the answer?

Teller's tip

Students might research some of the other colorful characters of the time—for example, Sam Steele, Jerry Potts, James Macleod, and George French of the NWMP; native leaders Crowfoot, Big Bear, Poundmaker, and Piapot; and villains Johnny Jerome Healey, Dave Akers, and Harry "Kamoose" Taylor.

Follow-up activities

- Draw a character-attribute web for Inspector Walsh.
- Native North Americans often used symbols or pictures to communicate. Have students draw some simple pictures related to the events in this story. Then have students use markers to draw the pictures on poster paper so they tell the story. (You might show students some authentic Indian pictographs before they begin drawing.)

Student Activity Sheet • Many Voices • Inspector Walsh and Sitting Bull

Name _____

Directions: Think about each problem and solution below. In the circles on the right, write what you believe the solution's effects would be on each party involved in the dispute. On the lines beneath, evaluate the solution, and offer an alternative if you think the problem could have been solved in a better way.

Problem and solution   **Effects**

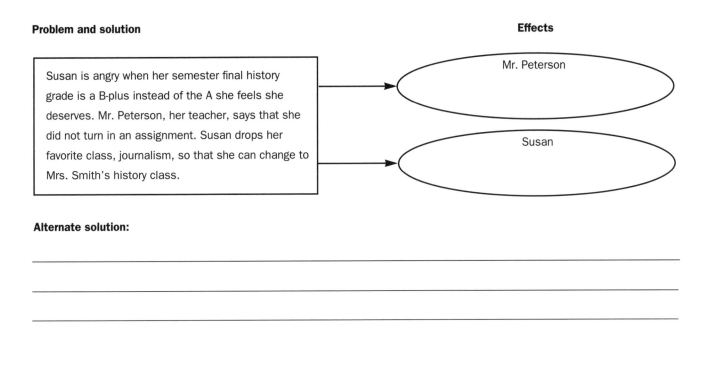

Susan is angry when her semester final history grade is a B-plus instead of the A she feels she deserves. Mr. Peterson, her teacher, says that she did not turn in an assignment. Susan drops her favorite class, journalism, so that she can change to Mrs. Smith's history class.

Mr. Peterson

Susan

Alternate solution:

_____

_____

_____

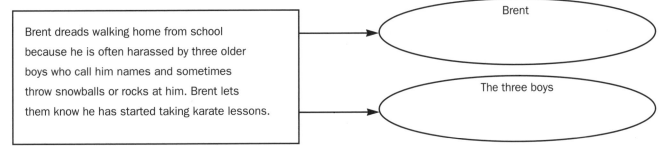

Brent dreads walking home from school because he is often harassed by three older boys who call him names and sometimes throw snowballs or rocks at him. Brent lets them know he has started taking karate lessons.

Brent

The three boys

Alternate solution:

_____

_____

_____

After you have completed this page, create a problem for your classmates to discuss. As a class, try to reach an agreement on the best solutions to the problems posed to others.

Aunt Clara Brown

Kay Negash _____

Objective

Students should be able to 1) identify Clara Brown and 2) list some of the cruel realities of slavery. This story shows that no matter how poor people are or how hard their lives, they can always make room for kindness and generosity to others.

Background

To give students a better understanding of what it was like to be a slave in the American South, read them some entries from Mary Lyons's *Letters From a Slave Girl: The Story of Harriet Jacobs* (Scribner, 1992) or parts of the award-winning *To Be a Slave* by Julius Lester (Dial, 1968).

Initiating activity

Most students have probably seen tearful reunions of long-lost relatives on television. Discuss some of the ways people become separated from one another. Speculate on how people might use today's advanced communication methods to find a lost family member.

Discussion questions

1. Would you call slaveholders who wouldn't sell a child younger than age 10 humanitarians? Why or why not?
2. Why do you think religion was important to slaves? How do African-American churches serve their communities today?
3. Evaluate Mr. Smith as a slave-owner. Who do you think made the decision to sell the slaves after Mr. Smith died? Compare Mr. Smith with Mr. Brown.
4. Compare the feelings of Liza Jane, Clara, Richard, and Mr. Smith after Paulina Ann drowned. What do you think the adults said to Liza Jane? What do you think Mr. Smith said to Clara and Richard?
5. A slave's fate was controlled by others. How did others control the lives of the slaves in this story?
6. What major changes occurred in Clara's life when she arrived at the Brunners'?

Follow-up activities

- Make a list of the milestones in Aunt Clara's life—the events that changed the direction of her life. Make a timeline showing these events. Use clues from the story to arrive at approximate dates. Add a concurrent timeline showing milestones in American history that occurred during Clara's life.
- Write one of the speeches that might have been given about Aunt Clara Brown when she was designated an official Colorado pioneer. Your speech should tell how Aunt Clara exemplified the qualities necessary for one to receive such an honor.

Teller's tip

Read about and listen to early Gospel music—the kind Aunt Clara Brown would have heard and sung at church or at revivals.

Student Activity Sheet • Many Voices • Aunt Clara Brown

Name _____

Directions: The way our life turns out often depends on the kindness of others, on decisions we have no control over, or on pure coincidence. On the chart below, summarize how the actions listed affected Clara's life. Then indicate whether each action was an act of kindness (**K**), a decision made with no particular consideration for Clara (**D**), or a coincidence (**C**).

Action or event	Effect on Clara's life	K D C
Mr. and Mrs. Smith took Clara to church.		
Paulina Ann went swimming in the creek.		
Mr. Smith died.		
Clara's husband and son were sold down the river.		
Mary Prue gave Clara her freedom papers and a letter of recommendation.		
Becky Johnson told Clara she should open her own business.		
The wagon master took Clara to Denver.		
Friends in Colorado gave Clara a train ticket to Iowa.		

Launching a Scientist: Robert Goddard's First Attempt at Rocketry

Kendall Haven _____

Objective

Students should be able to 1) explain how young Robert Goddard used the scientific method to test his childhood experiments and 2) comprehend that it is through failure that scientists learn.

Background

Scientists and others who make discoveries or invent new computers, toys, and even recipes usually have in mind an idea of what they want to achieve. But a good deal of experimentation is usually necessary before the goal can be reached.

Words to know: thrust, lift

Teller's tip

This story centers around a young boy's unbridled enthusiasm for science experiments. Try to instill in your listeners Robert's sense of excited wonder. The dual counterpoints to Robert are his friend's doubting cynicism and his mother's frustration and concern.

Initiating activity

Ask the students to define and discuss gravity. You might have them stand on chairs and drop objects of various weights (for example, a pencil and a wad of paper) to review the fact that objects of different weights fall at the same speed. Have the students contribute some ideas on what they could do to the pencil or scrap of paper to help it overcome gravity and rise from the floor. (Example: Tie a helium balloon to the pencil.) Also ask them what it would take to lift a student off the floor.

Discussion questions

1. Does Percy Long give Bobby much support in his experiments? Can you name other scientists, inventors, and explorers who were laughed at? Did you ever invent or create something that others laughed at?
2. Why do you think human beings have always wanted to fly? How might they have gotten the idea? How are birds designed for flight?
3. How did the reactions of Bobby's mother and father differ? Who do you think handled the situation better?

Follow-up activities

- Research other early rocketry projects—such as Chinese rockets that used gunpowder and the efforts of Konstantin Tsiolkovsky, Hermann Oberth, and Werner von Braun. Find out how a rocket differs from a jet.
- Discuss how rockets have been important in the struggle for world power.

Student Activity Sheet • Many Voices • Launching a Scientist

Name _____

Directions: To learn more about air pressure, lift, and propulsion, try some of the experiments and activities described below. Record your results, and try to figure out why you got them.

1. Make a basic paper airplane. Throw it across the room. What propelled the airplane? Try bending the wings at various angles. What happens now? Add a paper clip to the tail or the nose. What happens now?

2. Cut a strip of paper about an inch wide and eight inches long. Hold one end between your forefinger and thumb, just under the edge of your lower lip. Blow straight out. The paper should rise.

3. Put a deflated balloon in an empty plastic soft-drink bottle with the open end of the balloon stretched over the mouth of the bottle. Try to blow up the balloon. Can anyone do it?

4. Fold an index card in half. Open the card and place it on a table or desk, close to the edge. The card should still have a bend in it. Blow air straight under the card. The card should flatten out.

5. Make your own rocket, using a paper-towel tube, a paper cone for the nose, and cardboard cutouts for the fins. Think of several ways you might launch your rocket. Write down the possibilities, and check with your teacher to make sure all the ways you've thought of are safe. Try out the methods, and record your results and what you learn from them.

The Year of the Turnip in Oklahoma

Fran Stallings _____

Objectives

Students should be able to 1) differentiate between needs and wants, 2) define the word *homesteaders*, 3) recount the hardships of Western settlers, and 4) recognize the relationship between weather and farming.

Background

The promise of free land lured countless settlers west in the late 1800s. Prospective homesteaders literally "ran" to the land they claimed.

> *Words to know:* tenant farm, homestead, dugout house, compost, drought

Initiating activity

Use a T-chart to compare needs and wants. Have students list some of each. Try to narrow the needs side down to the "bare necessities" of food, clothing, and shelter. Ask how much they think all three of these necessities could be scaled back from the level most of us enjoy today.

Discussion questions

1. Why was the land run such a golden opportunity for the Macmillans?
2. Most of the Oklahoma Territory was given to the Cherokee nation and other native tribes who were forcibly moved there in the early 1800s. What do you imagine they said when they saw or heard about the land run?
3. Where would the Macmillans' diet of biscuits, skim milk, and pickles fit into today's food pyramid? If you had to live on one meal over and over, what would it be?
4. Although the settlers who stayed in Oklahoma must have been very tired of turnips, what do you suppose they told themselves as the spring of 1891 approached?

Follow-up activities

- If one of your relatives had been part of a famous American event—the California gold rush, for instance, or the Johnstown flood of 1889—how would you go about gathering information to write a story?
- View the exciting land-run scene from the 1992 movie *Far and Away* with Tom Cruise and Nicole Kidman.

Teller's tip

It's amazing how many students don't know what turnips are. Try some of these hands-on activities: See and handle turnips; taste turnips (raw slices with salt are convenient and appealing); carve turnips for block printing; outline a large turnip on paper, and draw scenes from the story or write a poem within the shape.

Student Activity Sheet • Many Voices • The Year of the Turnip in Oklahoma

Name _____

Directions: You have only $12 to feed a family of four for two days. Your assignment is to design a nutritious, filling menu that won't exceed your budget. Listed below are some foods and prices. Plan your menus, and then check off the items for your shopping list. (You have on hand one quart of milk, butter, mayonnaise, salad dressing, jelly, spices, and sugar.)

__ potato chips, 4 servings, $1.39

__ corn-muffin mix, 12 muffins, 50 cents

__ pork chops, 4, $3.89

__ pinto beans, 2 cans (8 servings), 66 cents

__ candy bars, package of 6, $1.49

__ eggs, 1 dozen, 84 cents

__ bread, 1 loaf, 99 cents

__ porterhouse steak, 1¹/₂ lb., $7.89

__ milk, 1 gallon (16 cups), $1.69

__ soda pop, 12 cans, $3.49

__ grapefruit, 4, $1

__ oatmeal, 10 servings, $1.29

__ carrots, 1 lb., 59 cents

__ wheat flakes, 8 servings, 99 cents

__ orange juice, 8 servings, $1.79

__ apples, bag of 12, $1.39

__ lettuce, 1 head, 59 cents

__ rice, 1 lb. (12 servings), 49 cents

__ tomatoes, canned, 16 oz., 29 cents

__ peanut butter, 12 oz., $1.19

Menus

	Breakfast	**Lunch**	**Dinner**
Day 1			
Day 2			

What's left for snacks?

Zayde's Trunk

Karen Golden

Objective

Students should be able to give reasons for immigration to America in the past and now.

Background

By the late 1800s life for Russian Jews had become nearly intolerable. They were prevented from worshiping as they wanted and couldn't own land. And when Jewish boys became teens, many were forced to serve in the czar's army for as long as 25 years.

Words to know: bar mitzvah, steerage class, sweatshop, tallis

Initiating activities

• Read and discuss the following inscription (written by Emma Lazarus) from the Statue of Liberty:

> Give me your tired, your poor,
> Your huddled masses yearning to breathe free,
> The wretched refuse of your teeming shore,
> Send these, the homeless, tempest-tossed, to me:
> I lift my lamp beside the golden door.

• Ask students to brainstorm reasons why people see America as "the land of opportunity." Also discuss why it is often called "a nation of immigrants."

Discussion questions

1. Is Itzi's mother's advice to him typical of the advice most teenage boys get from their mothers? Is it like advice your mother would give you?
2. Are there countries today where innocent people might be arrested for no reason?
3. How was Itzi's bar mitzvah like and unlike one you might attend today? Was there any similar ritual for Jewish girls when they reached age 13? Is there today?
4. Why do you think American businessmen were glad to see the immigrants arrive? Is that still true today?
5. How does Itzi's story exemplify the American dream?
6. Why do you think Itzi decided to go back to New York?

Follow-up activities

• Ask Jewish students to share information on Jewish customs.
• Many students have stories to tell about relatives who immigrated to America from Europe. Invite them or their family members to share their stories.

Teller's tip

To re-create a sweatshop atmosphere, dump a mixture of dry beans, lentils, and rice into a large pot, and have students sort the items. Tell them that children in sweatshops worked up to 10 hours a day at equally boring tasks and that millions of children in some countries still do.

Student Activity Sheet • Many Voices • Zayde's Trunk

Name _____

Directions: Itzi spoke Yiddish when he left Russia. Like many other immigrants, he probably continued to use some Yiddish words even as he learned English. That's why so many Yiddish words have become common in American English.

The trunk pictured below is full of Yiddish, or "Yinglish," words that you may already know. Fill in the blanks in the sentences with words from the trunk that seem to fit. Look for contextual clues.

1. I don't want to _____ that heavy suitcase with me!

2. She's on some crazy _____ diet again.

3. I don't want to play cards. I'll just sit here and _____.

4. I don't know what's wrong with my computer. Some kind of _____, I guess.

5. What a terrible movie! The script was _____ _____ _____.

6. Straight A's? _____ _____!

7. He'll probably find some poor _____ to fall for his story.

8. I'm not really surprised he dropped his tie in his soup. He's always been kind of a _____.

9. Are you hungry? Want to _____? How about a _____ with cream cheese?

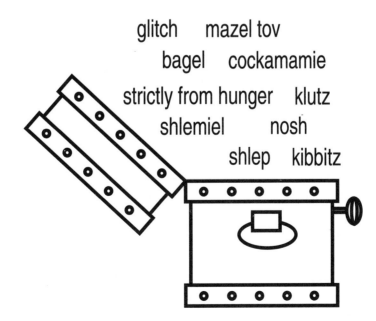

glitch   mazel tov
bagel   cockamamie
strictly from hunger   klutz
shlemiel   nosh
shlep   kibbitz

45

Scott Joplin: Master of Ragtime

Bobby Norfolk

Objectives

Students should be able to 1) identify Scott Joplin as the King of Ragtime, 2) describe ragtime music and explain when it became popular, and 3) recognize the importance of setting goals and working hard to reach them.

Background

This brief autobiography of Scott Joplin does not include the facts about his death. Joplin became so obsessed with the production of his opera, *Tremonisha*, that he had a nervous breakdown, for which he was institutionalized in 1916. He died the following year.

Words to know: ragtime, syncopation

Initiating activity

The best way to introduce Scott Joplin is with a recording of one of his most popular tunes, "The Entertainer." See if students can identify the type of music. Have them brainstorm to see how many musical styles they can list on the board, then compare some of the styles, for example, country and classical. How are they alike? Different? (You might use Venn diagrams for the comparisons.)

Discussion questions

1. In the late 1800s more and more American families began buying pianos for their homes. For what related product would there thus be an increased demand? How did Scott Joplin contribute to filling this demand?
2. Popular music is music that appeals to large numbers of people. What types of music would be considered popular music today? What do you think constituted popular music in 17th-century America? In the 1940s?
3. What does Scott Joplin's story tell you about the importance of setting a goal and trying your best to reach it? What short-term goals do you have? What long-range goals do you have—for example, what do you want to be doing when you're 25?
4. The music Scott Joplin heard in church had a big influence on him. Can you name some popular singers of today and recent years who got their start in church? If you can't think of any, where could you look to find out?
5. What inventions and changes have given modern adults and children entertainment choices different from those that were available in 1900?

Follow-up activities

• On your desk, try keeping time with your left hand and drumming out an uneven rhythm with your right hand. Is it harder than you thought it would be? What is the right-hand rhythm called?
• Allow students the opportunity to share their favorite music with the class. You might have a short "recital" by those who play instruments or sing, or you might play tapes or CDs students bring from home as background music during cleanup, journal writing, and other quiet activities.

Student Activity Sheet • Many Voices • *Scott Joplin: Master of Ragtime*

Name _____

Directions: To solve this crossword, you may need help from people of different ages who can tell you about the music that was popular when they were growing up.

Across

1. Scott Joplin was the King of _____.
3. "My Old _____ Home" is sung at an important horse race every year.
5. "When _____ Comes Marching Home" was a Civil War song.
7. "_____ the Beautiful"
9. M. C. Hammer and Tone Loc are _____.
12. "Unforgettable" was made popular by Nat King _____.
13. This "Fab Four" group shocked '60s parents with their "long" hair, but teens loved them.
14. Like 10 down, this is a stringed instrument.
15. Second word of 6 down.
16. Jazz great _____ Ellington.
17. Julia Ward Howe wrote "The Battle Hymn of the _____" after visiting a Union camp during the Civil War.
19. The great composer Ludwig van _____ became deaf at the height of his career.
20. Our national anthem is "The Star _____ Banner."

Down

2. Two words: Scott Joplin used this song title on his business card.
4. "Blowin' in the _____" was a song popular with people who opposed the Vietnam War.
5. Pearl _____, alternative rock musicians
6. First word of a song British soldiers sang to make fun of colonial Americans. We still sing it proudly today.
8. "____ _____ 'Tis of Thee"
10. Scott Joplin's instrument of choice
11. "I'm an old cowhand from the _____ Grande."
13. Country-music great Garth _____
15. A song Confederate soldiers sang about the land they called home
18. "The King of Rock and Roll," who some say is still alive

47

The Courage of Ed Pulaski

Jim Cogan

Objectives
Students should be able to 1) explain why Ed Pulaski is considered a hero and 2) describe the causes and effects of firestorms in forests.

Background
Resource books (see the list beginning on page 81) will help students picture the "ocean of forest" that makes up Idaho's Coeur d'Alene National Forest.

Words to know: conflagration, mattock, maelstrom, cannonade, firestorm, incinerate

Initiating activity
These simple demonstrations will show students how wind and air affect fire. 1. Light a votive candle. Hold a piece of crumpled paper near the flame but not near enough to ignite the paper. Then ask a student to blow sideways on the flame until it meets the paper and ignites it. 2. Relight the same candle. Lower a small clear drinking glass over the candle. Note that when the oxygen is used up, the flame dies. The point: Wind causes fire to spread, and fire needs oxygen to burn.

Discussion questions
1. Have you ever fallen in love with a place as Ed Pulaski did with the area where this story occurs? What do you like most about that place? What did you do while you were there? How would you feel if it were destroyed by fire?
2. Why was it so important for all the firefighters to work together? In what other situations and occupations is teamwork essential? In which ones is it unnecessary?
3. Why do you think the author used phrases such as "The end of the world had come to Idaho" and ". . . the terrible beauty of wildfire dancing . . ."?
4. Do you think Ed needed to resort to threatening George with his pistol? Why do you think he insisted that George come with the others? Why didn't he let him fend for himself? How else might he have handled the situation?
5. How is the courage of Ed Pulaski remembered by firefighters today?

Follow-up activities
- Locate the Coeur d'Alene National Forest near Wallace, Idaho, on a U.S. map. Locate the national or state forests nearest your community. Discuss the importance of setting aside land for wildlife. You might stage a debate or write essays about the conflict in the Pacific Northwest, where environmentalists and loggers disagree about what should be done with the last of the old-growth forest.
- Design posters or fliers that urge campers to take precautions with fire. These should be appropriate for placement at national and state forest campgrounds.
- Research an environmental figure such as John Muir, Marjorie Stoeman Douglas, or Anne LaBastille and an organization such as the Sierra Club, the National Audubon Society, the Nature Conservancy, or the National Wildlife Federation.

Student Activity Sheet • Many Voices • *The Courage of Ed Pulaski*

Name _____

Directions: Fill in the graphic below. Then use your notes to write a character sketch of a person—real or imaginary—who is a hero to you.

Words that describe heroes

What heroes do

Examples of heroic deeds

How society treats its heroes

How heroes feel afterward

The Laundry Man
Who Overthrew the Qing Dynasty

Charlie Chin

Objectives

Students should be able to 1) identify Sun Yat-sen, 2) examine various kinds of gifts and reasons for giving them, and 3) list their U.S. senators and representative and write to them about an issue that interests the students.

Background

Documented Chinese civilization began with the Shang dynasty (c. 1523–1027 B.C.). A dynasty was a period during which the country was ruled by a succession of monarchs from the same family. The final dynasty, the Ch'ing (Qing), or Manchu, lasted from 1644 to 1912. Dr. Sun Yat-sen was a revolutionary leader whose political theories were instrumental in the overthrow of that dynasty.

Words to know: dynasty, empress

Initiating activity

Ask the students how many of them have given money to support a cause they believe in. List some of these causes on the board. Then elicit suggestions for a list of students' most valuable possessions—for example, a computer, a CD collection, or savings bonds. Would any of the causes on the first list warrant giving up those things? (Example: Would you donate your computer if it would help end illiteracy in your community?) Generate a third list of causes worthy of such large gifts. Finally, discuss nonmaterial "gifts" students can give in order to promote the things they believe in—writing letters to elected officials, walking dogs at the humane society, reading to the elderly, etc.

Discussion questions

1. What did you learn from this story that you didn't know before?
2. The narrator states that the story is a "legend based on historical fact." How much of the story is historical fact, and how much is legend?
3. What does this story have to say about the meaning of a gift from the heart? What is the narrator saying about patriotism, honesty, and weakness?
4. Suppose you could donate $1 million to your community or your country. What instructions would you give for its use? Do you think your donation would be used exactly as you instructed?

Follow-up activities

- Describe a time you received (or gave) a very special gift.
- Use magazine cutouts, sketches, words, and small objects to make a collage of gifts you would like to give to a friend—or that you would like to receive yourself. (The items need not be material things alone.)
- Use reference books in your library to find out what others have said about gifts. Collect some favorite quotations and make a poster to display them.

Student Activity Sheet • Many Voices • *The Laundry Man Who Overthrew the Qing Dynasty*

Name _____

Directions: Almost everyone finds time to complain about what happens in the Congress, but many don't take the time to vote, and even fewer call or write their representatives to let them know how they feel. For this activity you will need several recent newspapers and a phone book.

1. Scan the newspapers for articles about legislation that the Congress is considering. Some bills may be before the House, some before the Senate. Some issues may be in the discussion stage, with no bills proposed yet. Find the issue or bill you feel is the most important. Summarize it below:

2. Consult your phone book for the names, addresses, and phone and fax numbers of your senators and representative. If an electronic-mail address is listed, include it too.

Senator _____
Address: _____
City: _____ State: _____ ZIP: _____
Phone: _____ Fax: _____
E-mail: _____

Senator _____
Address: _____
City: _____ State: _____ ZIP: _____
Phone: _____ Fax: _____
E-mail: _____

Representative _____
Address: _____
City: _____ State: _____ ZIP: _____
Phone: _____ Fax: _____
E-mail: _____

3. Finally, write a letter stating your opinions and feelings about the issue you summarized above. Include valid reasons and/or examples to support your opinion. Copy the letter twice so that you can send it to all three congressional officials. (Be sure to change the name and address at the top of each.) Mail, fax, or e-mail your letters. Later, with your class, share your original letter and the responses you receive.

Stagecoach Mary

Sharon Y. Holley

Objectives

Students should be able to 1) identify Mary Fields as the first African-American woman to drive a stagecoach for the U.S. Post Office and 2) compare and contrast Mary's acts of kindness with acts showing her tough character.

Background

Stagecoaches provided cheap transportation to the West, although they were decidedly uncomfortable and often the target of outlaws. Stagecoaches also carried the mail, texts of presidents' speeches, and other important news from the East.

After the Civil War many former slaves did not find themselves in much better condition financially or socially. They worked for poor wages or on tenant farms and were terrorized by resentful groups of whites such as the Ku Klux Klan. The West offered them hope. As an 1879 Kansas newspaper, *The Colored Citizen*, declared, "It is better to starve in Kansas than be shot and killed in the South."

Words to know: entrepreneurial spirit

Initiating activity

Most students have seen stagecoaches in Western movies or television programs. Have them formulate a job description for the stagecoach driver. Ask: If you were doing the hiring, would you hire a woman to drive your stagecoach?

Discussion questions

1. What are some possible reasons why there is little information about Mary Fields's birth and early life? How could someone find out when you were born and where you went to grade school?
2. After reading Mary's description, how do you think you would feel if you were introduced to her? Would you find her intimidating? Interesting? Kind?
3. In spite of her appearance and ability to be tough when necessary, what evidence do you have of Mary's essentially kind nature?
4. Did Mary seem to be affected by racism? Why or why not? To what do you attribute her popularity with the residents of Cascade?

Follow-up activities

- Make up an anecdote about Mary that is not mentioned in the story but that could have happened. Choose an appropriate spot in the story to place your anecdote.
- With a partner, write a rap song about Mary Fields's life, and present it to your class.
- Analyze Mary's character by finding evidence in the story that she was loyal, dependable, kind, tough, well-liked, and imposing.

Teller's tip

Have students design a postage stamp for Stagecoach Mary. Then prepare a ceremony or program to unveil the stamps.

Student Activity Sheet • Many Voices • Stagecoach Mary

Name _____

Directions: Below is a blank front page of the *Cascade Courier*, published soon after Mary Fields's death. Write a brief obituary. Add an interview with Mother Amadeus. (We'll assume she was able to come to the funeral.) Use your imagination to fill in the blanks with articles, advertisements, a cartoon, a horoscope, or other items that might have appeared in a small-town Montana newspaper in the early 1900s.

Cascade Courier
All the news that's fit
Mary Fields Dies at 81

Memories of Mary

The Horse That Went to War

Sheila Dailey _____

Objectives

Students should be able to 1) explain the part Canada played in the First World War and 2) analyze the importance of personal sacrifice for a greater good.

Background

On June 28, 1914, Archduke Francis Ferdinand, heir to the Austro-Hungarian throne, was assassinated by a Serbian nationalist. Austria-Hungary declared war on Serbia, and France, Great Britain, the United States, and Russia (the Allied Powers) ultimately joined forces against Austria-Hungary, which was joined by Germany and Turkey (the Central Powers). Canada, then ruled by Great Britain, joined the Allied forces.

Words to know: maternal and paternal grandparents, dour

Teller's tip

The story is bittersweet, and listeners need time to digest it before you launch into discussion. One way to do that might be to show listeners the picture and point out what kinds of information the photo gives us, noting such things as dress and time of year.

Initiating activity

Discuss the concept of sacrifice. Write the word in large block letters on a butcher-paper easel or on the chalkboard. Ask a student to jot notes around the word as you elicit answers to the following questions: In what situation might you decide to sacrifice your time for someone else? For what cause or person would you give up a week's allowance? Would you give your dog to Leader Dogs for the Blind? What is the "ultimate sacrifice" asked of soldiers? How can the people back home help a war effort? Have you ever done anything to help during a war?

Discussion questions

1. What kinds of friendship does this story explore? Have you ever been friends with someone like Dirty Billy?
2. Do you consider any animals your friends? What special qualities do animals have that make them good companions? Have you ever been friends with a horse?
3. Do you think it was fair for Evelyn's grandmother to ask her to give up Big Jim? What might have happened if Evelyn had refused? What would you have done in her place?
4. What did Evelyn learn about herself and the world by giving up Big Jim?
5. What do you think happened to Big Jim?

Follow-up activities

- Locate the Bruce Peninsula, a long finger of land to the southeast of the Georgian Bay of Lake Huron. Note that this is still a popular recreation area. Have students speculate about what it might be like to live there year-round now.
- Ask students to bring in old black-and-white photos from home that have stories behind them. Have students briefly tell the stories as they share the photos.

Student Activity Sheet • Many Voices • *The Horse That Went to War*

Name _____

Directions: Imagine that Evelyn's class decided to sell buttons to raise money and to encourage people to help Canada's soldiers in World War I. With a partner, brainstorm some ideas for things that children and adults back home could do to show their support and to make life easier for the soldiers. Choose the four ideas you think are best, and design buttons in the space below.

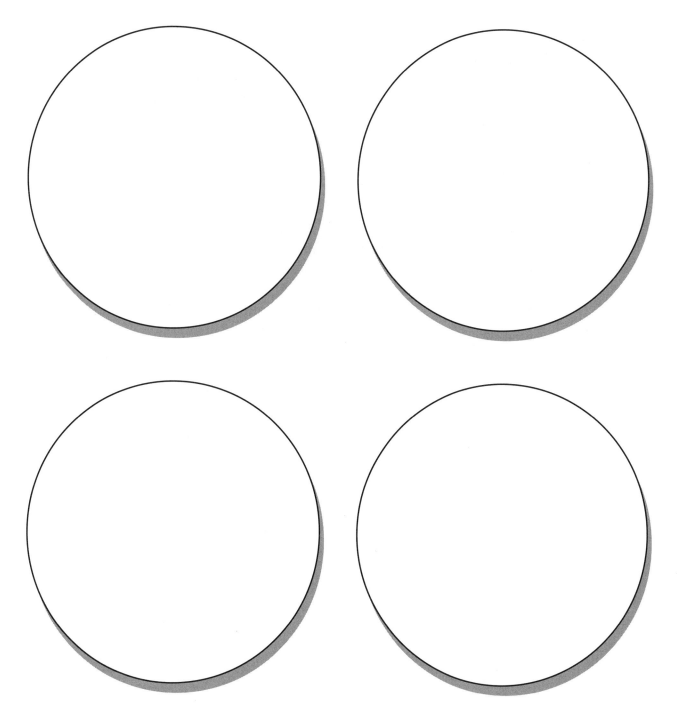

Say Goodbye to Papa:
The Regina Sinreich Barton Story

Annette Harrison

Objectives
Students should be able to 1) list motives for immigration to the United States in the early 1900s, 2) assess the effects of poor working and living conditions on families, and 3) analyze the importance of cooperation within a family to attain a better life for all.

Background
By the early 1900s Americans were changing from producers to consumers. With the demand high for factory-produced goods of all kinds, American businessmen sought a cheap source of labor. Agricultural failures, political unrest, and ethnic and religious discrimination brought many Europeans to America where they could easily find work in factories and hoped to enjoy a life free of persecution.

Words to know: tuberculosis, tenement

Initiating activities
- America has often been called a melting pot, but some people say it is more like a salad bowl. Which term do you think is more appropriate?
- America's promise of prosperity and freedom appealed to both the Founding Fathers and the immigrants in this story. What did the two groups have in common? In what ways were they, and conditions in America when they arrived, different?

Discussion questions
1. Was it worthwhile for Regina's family to come to America?
2. Does the voyage in the story remind you of the journey of any groups coming into America today? How do many Cubans, Haitians, and Mexicans enter the country?
3. Who, if anyone, was to blame for Papa's illness and eventual death? How are workers protected from sweatshop working conditions today?
4. Should the United States restrict immigration more than it already does? Why are some people angry about the number of immigrants who arrive here each year?
5. What insight does this story give on the need for unions and child-labor laws?

Follow-up activities
- Find out the nationalities of those who came to your community from other countries in the 1900s. You might investigate primary documents such as old newspapers; records of births, marriages, and deaths; and land records. A county historian may be willing to talk to your class about immigration to your area as well, and older residents may have information they would enjoy sharing.
- Draw "before" and "after" pictures of Papa: before he left for America and after four years of working in the factory.

Teller's tip
Have the students create a letter from a child in the old country to a parent in America, Regina's journal entry written aboard ship, or a story from a bedbug's point of view.

Student Activity Sheet • Many Voices • *Say Goodbye to Papa*

Name _____

Directions: At about the time of this story, many new products were being produced that middle-class people could buy: cameras, record players, radios, and even automobiles. We often think of the person who can "build a better mousetrap" as one who will become a success. Inventing something that worked well and became popular often meant wealth and fame for the inventor.

1. Consider some common object in your home that is used nearly every day: a bathtub, a VCR, a dishwasher, or even something as simple as a clothes hanger. Write the name of your object here.

    _____

2. Think about what is wrong with or irritating or frustrating about the object. What are its drawbacks? Ask family members what they think too. Write your thoughts below.

    _____

    _____

    _____

    _____

3. Now it's time to build a better mousetrap. Redesign the object to eliminate the drawbacks you listed. Your design should include a sketch showing your improvements and a brief written explanation. If you need more room, use the back of your paper or a separate sheet.

Rider on an Orphan Train

David Massengill

Objectives

Students should be able to 1) compare treatment of and attitudes toward children at the beginning of the 20th century and now, 2) explain what "orphan trains" were, and 3) theorize their effects on the children who rode them.

Background

As the United States became more industrialized after the Civil War, thousands of immigrants, freed slaves, and others flocked to Northeastern cities to find the good life. Instead they drew only minimal wages for long hours of monotonous work and lived in slums where they were subject to disease and poor conditions. There were no child-labor laws, and children worked long hours in factories for wages even lower than those of adults. For various reasons—their parents' illness or death or simple desperation—a number of children in these slums were left to live on the streets.

Initiating activity

Discuss the abandonment of children—the legal delivery of children into foster care or adoption services as well as illegal abandonment, for example, leaving newborn babies in garbage cans or at hospitals. What are some reasons parents are unable or unwilling to take care of their children? What are some things that happen in our society to children who do not live with their parents? Under what circumstances is it better for children not to be with their parents? If you were abandoned but had a brother or sister with you, would your sibling seem more important to you than he or she had before? Why?

Discussion questions

1. For children on the orphan train, what would be the best and worst outcomes?
2. List some feelings you imagine the children had as the orphan train pulled into various stations along the way. Put yourself in the place of the families who came to meet the trains. What kinds of reasons would they have had for wanting to adopt one or more of the children?
3. Do you think Reverend Brace helped improve conditions for the children he tried to help, or would they have been better off left on their own? What probably would have happened to most of them if he had not tried to help?
4. Discuss cases like those of the famous "Baby Jessica," whose birth parents reclaimed her after she had been adopted, the twin girls who were separated in a divorce settlement so each parent could have custody of one of the girls, and the boy who "divorced" his real parents so he could live with his foster family.

Follow-up activities

- Work in small groups to create a "bill of rights for children."
- Have one group of students role-play the scene on the day an orphan train arrives in a small town in Nebraska or Kansas. Other groups can show what happens at the new homes of several of the adopted children.

Student Activity Sheet • Many Voices • Rider on an Orphan Train

Name _____

Directions: David Massengill's song is written as a series of quatrains—four lines of verse. In his song the first and second lines rhyme, and the third and fourth lines rhyme. This is called an AABB rhyme scheme.

Using the song as a model, write a poem about someone you used to know but haven't seen for a long while and don't know how to contact. You might want to add a happy ending to your poem—for example, you get a letter or phone call from your long-lost friend or relative. If this situation doesn't apply to you, you might want to put yourself in the place of one of the orphans on the train. Write about how you came to be on the train and where you finally ended up.

_____

_____

_____

_____

_____

_____

_____

_____

_____

_____

_____

_____

_____

_____

_____

_____

_____

_____

_____

_____

_____

The Herring Shed

Jay O'Callahan

Objectives

Students should be able to 1) assess the importance of community during times of crisis as well as normal life and 2) identify unique and common characteristics of rural and urban life.

Background

Canada was allied with Great Britain, the United States, and France in World War II. This story takes place in Nova Scotia, a Canadian province. (Locate Nova Scotia, Cape Tormentine, and the Northumberland Strait on a map of North America.) Ask students to speculate on the occupations of people in this province, particularly those living in small coastal villages. Mining, farming, fishing, and fish-processing are primary occupations.

Words to know: gill, rector, Dunkirk (a battle in which many lives were lost)

Initiating activity

Every year tornadoes, hurricanes, earthquakes, floods, famines, and other disasters occur. Have the students think about television coverage they have seen of such events. How do the members of the affected communities handle these crises? Do students agree that a disaster brings out the best in people?

Discussion questions

1. What can be accomplished when the members of a community work together? Describe a time when you pitched in with a group to get something done.
2. Find examples in this story of how people use humor to alleviate pain and grief. What other coping methods do the characters use when they learn of the deaths of Harry, Jack, and Gannett?
3. This story covers one year. Does the narrator, Maggie Thomas, change during that year? How? What does she learn about herself and her community?
4. Why does Charlie Robertson appear in this story? What kind of feeling do you get about the residents—named and unnamed—of Cape Tormentine? Would you like to have them for neighbors?
5. What does this story have to say about wealth—economic as well as spiritual? Which is more important to Maggie?

Follow-up activity

Choose several rhythmic passages from the story, and read them as a group.

Teller's tip

Sit in a circle and do some repetitive task. For example, demonstrate a simple process to be done with a book: open the book, close the book, turn it over, and pass it on. Make up a simple rhythm to match the task, and chant together as you pass the book around. Discuss the fact that over the centuries sailors invented and sang rhythmic sea chanteys to help make their tasks—for instance, pulling in sails—easier.

Student Activity Sheet • Many Voices • *The Herring Shed*

Name _____

Directions: Maggie worked in the herring shed under a piecework system, in which she got paid according to how much work she did. Most workers today receive hourly wages or annual salaries.

In small-group discussion, consider the two systems from the viewpoints of both the employee and the employer. List advantages and disadvantages. Take a vote within your group on the best system to work under if you are an employee. Take another vote on which system is best for the employer. Record the results for each item. A group spokesperson should summarize your discussion and report the voting results. Votes for the whole class can then be tallied.

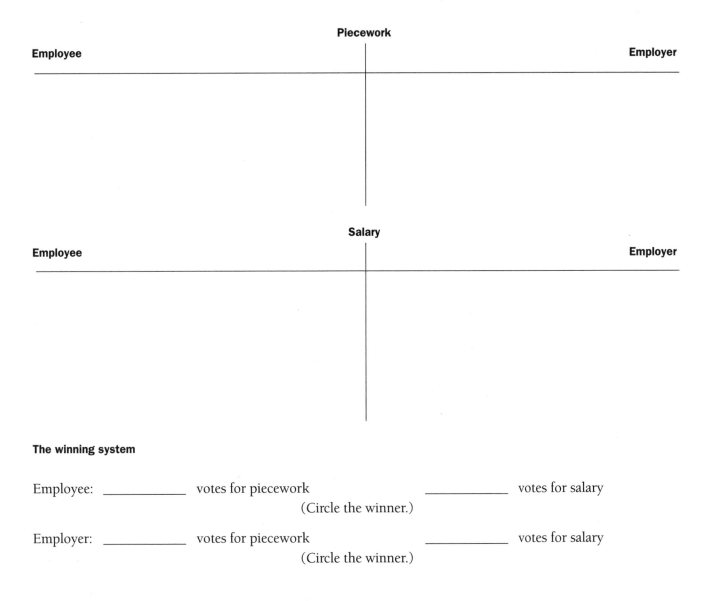

Piecework

Employee   **Employer**

Salary

Employee   **Employer**

The winning system

Employee: _____ votes for piecework   _____ votes for salary
                              (Circle the winner.)

Employer: _____ votes for piecework   _____ votes for salary
                              (Circle the winner.)

Rosie the Riveter

Judith Black _____

Objectives

Students should be able to 1) evaluate the short- and long-term effects of women's entering the assembly line in 1944 and 2) identify instances of sexism and racism in the story and make correlations with their existence in today's world.

Background

Throughout history women have had fewer rights and opportunities than men. Until quite recently women were excluded from professional jobs other than teaching and nursing, with few exceptions. Even today the great majority of employed women work in low-paying clerical, retail sales, and service jobs.

Words to know: prototype, Holocaust, sexism, racism

Teller's tip

Each Rosie embodies a different issue that women on the assembly lines struggled with. Rosie McRivet is doubted and chided for no other reason than her sex. The second Rosie deals with the Holocaust and the fact that many people refused to believe that the planned annihilation of a race was taking place in Europe. The third Rosie exposes the moral wound of American racism.

Initiating activity

Ask students to list women they have seen working in the past week. The list might include their own mothers, women at school, and women they see on television. Ask them what they think of when they hear the phrase *women's work*. Explain that they will hear a story about a prototype of a woman who surprised people during World War II.

Discussion questions

1. What important contributions did "the Rosies" of World War II make to the women's movement in general?
2. Find examples of racism and sexism in the story. What makes such language offensive? Do you think men in a similar situation today would treat women the same way?
3. Were Rosella's actions correct? Is the threat of violence a good way to solve problems?
4. Which Rosie would be the most likely to become a factory supervisor? To become a civil-rights lawyer? To open a restaurant of her own?
5. Some political analysts claim that "angry white males" now make up another "special-interest group." How do you suppose a member of this group would react to this story?

Follow-up activities

- Write another verse for the poem about Rosie, following the same format.
- Find out what is meant by the term *the glass ceiling*.
- Bring in and discuss articles about events involving racism, sexism, affirmative action, and women in the workplace.

Student Activity Sheet • Many Voices • *Rosie the Riveter*

Name _____

Directions: Choose the story of one of the three Rosies. With a partner, rewrite the events and dialogue the way they might occur in a similar setting today, for instance at an auto-assembly plant. You can add characters to the section of the story you choose, add other events, or even add a sequel. (For example, Rosie McRivet might decide to file sexual-harassment charges against "the boys," Rosie Rivitchsky might share a video of *Schindler's List* with her co-workers, and Rosella Riveton might contact the American Civil Liberties Union for help with the problems caused by the set-up man.)

Rosie _____'s story

_____

_____

_____

_____

_____

_____

_____

_____

_____

_____

_____

_____

_____

_____

_____

_____

_____

_____

_____

Such Things to Write About

Paul Q. Lipman and Doug Lipman _____

Objectives

Students should be able to 1) compare and contrast the perspectives of the stereotypical professional soldier and a nonprofessional soldier and 2) explain the irony in this story.

Background

For thousands of years letters were the primary means of communication between people. Today many of us are more likely to pick up the phone or send an e-mail message or a fax. Many families have saved letters from relatives. These letters give later generations a special insight into the personalities and lives of grandparents, great-grandparents, aunts, uncles, and other relatives they have never met.

Initiating activity

Ask the students to share photocopies of letters their families have saved. Letters written during wars are especially appropriate, but any letters that students bring in can be used to point out how precious such documents become over time. Have the students give some background: who wrote the letter, where it was written, who received it, why it was saved, and whether the student ever met the writer of the letter or its recipient.

Discussion questions

1. How was Virginia and Paul's marriage "a step toward peace"? Do you agree that "love and beauty and peace don't have any religion or race"?
2. Does Paul fit your image of the courageous World War II soldier? Do you think most soldiers today feel like Paul did?
3. How might a "red-letter day" for a general be different from the one Paul describes?
4. What perspective on "the important things in life" does Paul gain from his war experience? Make a list of the simple things you are grateful for.
5. From Paul's descriptions of the concentration camp, do you think war had hardened him to the suffering of others? Is that something that necessarily happens to soldiers?
6. What is ironic about the actions of Paul's father and the fact that Paul is fighting a war to liberate those who do not fit the Nazis' definition of "superpeople"?

Follow-up activity

Discuss the kinds of marriages that parents today would consider unsuitable. Ask students if they think "true love" is all that is needed to overcome obstacles interracial and interreligious couples face. What problems does society present to such couples?

Tellers' tip

Have the students create fictional letters. Suggestions include the response of Paul's father to the letter Paul finally wrote him; Virginia's response to any of the letters; Virginia's description of V-E day in Michigan City; the French woman's letter to her sons, describing the American soldiers' arrival; and a letter written by one of the concentration-camp inmates, describing the day the Americans arrived.

Student Activity Sheet • Many Voices • Such Things to Write About

Name _____

Directions:

1. As in Paul's case, parents and children often have different ideas about who makes an ideal mate. Use the Venn diagram below to show how your ideas differ from those of your parents and how they are similar. Under *My ideal*, write some characteristics of the person you'd consider the perfect boyfriend or girlfriend. Under *Parents' ideal*, write characteristics of the person they would choose for you. Where the circles overlap, write characteristics you and your parents agree on.

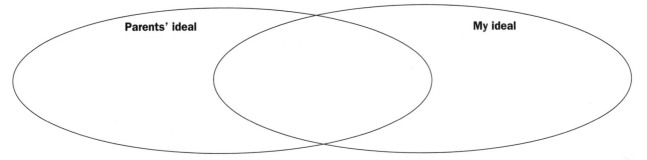

Parents' ideal   **My ideal**

2. Suppose you marry your "perfect person" and your parents, like Paul's father, stop speaking to you. What are some possible actions you could take? List them below. Weigh each action against the criteria listed on the chart below by answering yes, no, or maybe.

Criteria

	Will I feel better if I do this?	Will this bring the family back together?	Will this cause more problems?
Possible actions _____ _____ _____ _____ _____ _____ _____ _____ _____			

The Garbage Story

Susan "Supe" O'Halloran

Objectives

Students should be able to 1) define and discuss racism, 2) analyze sources of negative stereotypes, 3) get a sense of the turbulence of the 1960s, and 4) formulate possible solutions for social change.

Background

After World War II ended, America enjoyed an unprecedented era of economic boom as a result of industrial development. The dream of having a house and a yard became a reality for many families as their improved financial positions allowed them to move to the suburbs—areas where new houses were springing up at the edges of or outside cities. These areas were usually all-white.

Words to know: liberal, racist, prejudice

Initiating activity

Play some of the following songs from the '60s: "We Shall Overcome," "Blowin' in the Wind," "The Times They Are A-Changin'," "Black Day in July," and "Eve of Destruction." Ask students to listen closely to the lyrics. What points do the singers seem to be trying to make? How is this music like or unlike popular music today? (Many popular groups warn about damage to the environment, the dangers of drugs, and the senselessness of violence in social-protest songs.) What is the difference between accepting the status quo and trying to change society for the better? What is an activist?

Discussion questions

1. Sue's neighbors thought they had evidence for their beliefs about African-Americans. What were these beliefs, and what evidence did Sue find that explained why her neighbors were wrong?
2. Why do many people fear social and economic equality?
3. Have you kept quiet when you disagreed about a social or political issue? Why is it sometimes scary to state an opinion that others around you will disagree with?
4. Does the "porch for all of us to sit on" exist? How can we find it or create it?

Follow-up activity

Using magazine cutouts, original sketches, and other materials, make collages showing 1) the contrast between life in an urban ghetto and in an affluent suburb or 2) the contrast between the life of a teenage girl in the '50s and of a teenage girl today.

Teller's tip

What stereotypes did Sue's neighbors have about African-Americans? Where did they get these ideas? Ask: What stereotypes have you been taught? How do the media perpetuate racial stereotypes today?

Student Activity Sheet • Many Voices • *The Garbage Story*

Name _____

Directions: The narrator of this story was born in 1950, making her a baby boomer, one of a large group of people born after World War II. Many baby boomers reacted against the conform-to-the-norm expectations of the 1950s by "dropping out" of the social mainstream or by becoming activists: people who actively spoke out against things they believed were wrong with society.

Find a baby boomer who is willing to talk to you about what it was like to grow up in the '50s and '60s. Below are some suggested questions to ask your interviewee. You can add other questions to the list. Try to tape-record or videotape the interview so it can be easily shared with the class. After class members have shared their interview information, discuss this era in history. What good things came out of this chaotic period? What bad things resulted? In general, did the baby boomers do more good than harm or more harm than good? What conclusions, if any, can you draw about the baby boomers as adults?

Suggested interview questions
1. Did you grow up in the suburbs, the city, or a small town? How do you think the cities changed when many people moved to the suburbs? What was the dream of those who moved? What was it like for those left behind in the cities?
2. How did television shows such as *Ozzie and Harriet*, *Father Knows Best*, *Leave It to Beaver*, and *American Bandstand* affect your behavior or the way you dressed and wore your hair?
3. What do you remember about the Beatles? What were some of your favorite music groups and singers? What were protest songs like?
4. Did you ever participate in a demonstration? What did people demonstrate about during the '60s and early '70s? What "cause" would make you want to join a demonstration today?
5. What do you remember about the summer of 1967, when riots and fires ravaged dozens of U.S. cities?
6. What do you know about the Civil Rights Act of 1964? The Job Corps? Head Start?

An Orange

Joel ben Izzy

Objectives

Students should be able to interpret and explain the symbolic importance of the orange in this story.

Background

Most students will probably be familiar with the horrors of the Holocaust and with Auschwitz as one of the most notorious concentration camps. This story deals with human life—how precious it is, how suddenly it can be snuffed out—and with the appreciation of life and freedom that one man gains after being passed over by the arbitrary hand of death. The lesson inherent in this story for today's young people is that we should be grateful for the freedom we have to live our lives.

Initiating activity

Bring in enough oranges for the class to share. Write the word *orange* on the board. Pass the oranges around. Ask the students to concentrate on the attributes of an orange, and list descriptive words and phrases on the board. Try to make sure there are words related to the smell, feel, taste, texture, size, and weight of the orange. Then ask the students to describe a situation in which a simple orange could take on a great deal of meaning.

Discussion questions

1. Did the narrator seem irritated when the old man sat next to him on the bus? Do you think he was glad afterward? What did he learn from the story the old man told him?

2. Do you think the old man should have told the other prisoners about finding the orange? Should he have shared it with them? What do you think you would have done if you had been in his position?

3. Do you think it is possible for us to understand what it was like to be in a Nazi concentration camp? Have most of us experienced anything even remotely like it? Can you think of anything to compare it with?

4. What did the old man mean when he said, "The orange saved my life"? Was the orange's effect physical, emotional, or spiritual? What did the orange symbolize?

5. What advice do you imagine the old man would have given if the narrator had told him how he hated riding the bus and wished he had a car?

Follow-up activities

- Eat the oranges you handed out. Ask students to imagine that this is the only orange they will ever have or eat. Ask them to try to taste the orange from the old man's perspective. How is this orange different from others you have eaten without thinking about them?

- The memberships of neo-Nazi and white supremacist groups are growing. Discuss their beliefs and aims, and ask students to form and express their own opinions about such groups and the dangers they pose in a free society. Older students might research anti-Semitism throughout history.

Student Activity Sheet • Many Voices • *An Orange*

Name _____

Directions: Write about a time when you were depressed or felt hopeless but there was a "bright spot," like the old man's orange, that pulled you through. Perhaps someone you care about gave you some good advice or you spent time with a favorite pet, in a special place outdoors, or participating in a sport or other leisure activity. Try to describe your mood before and after the "bright spot" cheered you up.

_____

_____

_____

_____

_____

_____

_____

_____

_____

_____

_____

_____

_____

_____

_____

_____

_____

_____

_____

_____

_____

_____

Snapshot, 1944

David Mas Masumoto

Objectives

Students should be able to 1) explain what happened to Japanese-Americans under Executive Order 9066 and 2) analyze the effects that segregation and hostility had on the Japanese interned in "relocation centers."

Background

After the Japanese attack on Pearl Harbor in December 1941 anti-Japanese sentiment became rampant hostility. Executive Order 9066 provided for the relocation of 120,000 Japanese-Americans living in strategic areas of the West Coast. These citizens lost their homes, businesses, land, and legal rights and were treated as enemies. Ironically, the 442nd Regimental Combat Unit, made up of second-generation Japanese-Americans, became the most decorated Army unit of its size in American history.

Initiating activities

- Before telling or reading the story, discuss segregation—voluntary as well as forced—of various groups of people in the United States (Native Americans on reservations, blacks in ghettos, ethnic neighborhoods in cities, etc.). Elicit prior knowledge about the Japanese internment and discuss why many Americans at the time felt the move was justified.
- Display some photos of the faces of elderly people. Ask students to "read" the faces and to theorize about what kinds of lives the people have had.

Discussion questions

1. What is especially ironic about the death of the soldier in this story and the location of his funeral?
2. Why do you think *Baachan* insists the farm is hers and *Jiichan's*? Why does she tell the narrator's mother, "You kicked me out of my home. I have no home"? Who does she think the narrator's mother is?
3. *Baachan's* living son mumbles, "What was I supposed to say?" What do people usually say at funerals? Is there any way to comfort a mother who has lost a son or a wife who has lost a husband?
4. *Baachan* seems to feel that everything of value has been taken from her, and now she is just waiting to die. What advice would you like to give her?

Follow-up activities

- A Buddhist book begins with the sentence "All we are is the result of what we have thought." Discuss.
- Evaluate the controversy surrounding the Enola Gay exhibit at the Smithsonian Institution's National Air and Space Museum. Veterans protested that the exhibit as proposed portrayed the bombing of Hiroshima as an aggressive and unfeeling act against innocent people, whereas supporters of the exhibit claimed it should make a judgment on the morality of the decision to drop the bomb. What do you think?

Student Activity Sheet • Many Voices • Snapshot, 1944

Name _____

Directions: You may have eaten tofu, sushi, yakitori, or tempura, and you have probably ridden in a Toyota, a Honda, or a Suzuki. Many Japanese words are used every day in the English language. Similarly, many English words have entered the Japanese language. *Baachan* calls a bicycle a *bai-ku* and a book a *buu-ku*.

See how many Japanese *tangos* (words) you can match with their English equivalents. Have fun saying the words out loud.

	Japanese		English
____ 1.	Pepushi Kora	A.	engine
____ 2.	asuparagasu	B.	pineapple
____ 3.	jerii	C.	gasoline
____ 4.	futtoboru	D.	basketball
____ 5.	sandoicchi	E.	businessman
____ 6.	gasorin	F.	Pepsi Cola
____ 7.	kii	G.	dollar
____ 8.	doru	H.	giraffe
____ 9.	apato	I.	asparagus
____10.	jirafu	J.	cheese
____11.	basukettoboru	K.	sandwich
____12.	korekushon	L.	key
____13.	tosuta	M.	apartment
____14.	painappuru	N.	hot dog
____15.	aisu kuriimu	O.	milk
____16.	supagetti	P.	jelly
____17.	hotto doggu	Q.	correction
____18.	miruku	R.	football
____19.	chiizu	S.	spaghetti
____20.	bijinesuman	T.	toaster
____21.	enjin	U.	ice cream

Over the next few days, list Japanese words as you come across them.

Precious Freedom

Hanna Bandes Geshelin _____

Objectives

Students should be able to 1) identify and discuss the differences between democracies and totalitarian states and in the amount of personal freedom their citizens have and 2) explain the importance of guarding personal and political freedoms.

Background

Freedom is a precious word to Americans. We know it is something to value and protect, but to really understand what freedom is, we need to know its opposite. Brainstorm how communism affects the daily lives of those who live under it: the lack of a justice system, religious persecution, a poor standard of living, and constant fear that the secret police are listening, watching, and ready to apprehend blameless citizens.

Initiating activity

Ask the students: Imagine you are on a camping trip with your family, but when you get to the park, your family's car is searched, and you are all sent to separate prison camps with no explanation. How would it feel to escape to a country where you could be sure this would never happen? Would you ever forget the experience or stop being grateful for your new home?

Discussion questions

1. Tanya and the narrator were both immigrants of a sort. How was Tanya's experience of coming to America similar to the narrator's experience of moving from a small town to Boston? How were their experiences different? Where could you go inside this country but feel like an immigrant? Why?

2. People who live in foreign countries often think of America as a place where the shelves overflow with food. Is it true that no one goes hungry in America? Do you think people in other countries think of Americans as fat and well-fed? What other stereotypical images do you think they have?

3. What valuable gift does the narrator, in her anecdote, give Tanya and her guests? What do the Russians, in return, give back to the narrator? Do most people view the influx of immigrants to the United States as a reminder of our freedoms, or do they have other ideas?

4. This story is about learning lessons from the past—and not forgetting them. What unforgettable lessons have you learned? Have your parents or other relatives passed on any lessons to you from their experiences?

Follow-up activity

Create an illustrated booklet of examples of freedoms Americans enjoy. Use original sketches or pictures cut from magazines and newspapers. Captions for the pictures might be phrases from the Declaration of Independence, famous quotes, lines from songs, etc.

Student Activity Sheet • Many Voices • *Precious Freedom*

Name _____

Directions: *Americana* refers to a tradition, event, institution, idea, place, or custom uniquely representative of American society and culture. You will find Americana all around you at theme parks, fast-food establishments, supermarkets, baseball games, and shopping malls.

Imagine that you have recently become friends with a person about your age whose family has just immigrated to America. You have invited your friend to accompany you to a place where he or she will be exposed to plenty of Americana, and on your way there, you want to explain a little bit about what to expect. Write your explanation in narrative form, or create a dialogue between yourself and your friend.

Answer Key

Anne Hutchinson

Discussion questions: 1. She felt the Holy Spirit was a friend and that faith alone could lead to salvation. The Puritans felt good works "earned" salvation—although they also believed in predestination, so if a person was born condemned, he or she would stay that way no matter what. 2. Although Puritans forbade women to preach, Anne probably thought the governor would consider a woman's talking to other women as inconsequential. 3. Confess to heresy. 4. He wanted more people to help him fight the Indians. 5. Wampage felt he had to avenge the deaths of his Indian brothers and sisters.

Activity sheet: Top—Anne Hutchinson: Saw Holy Spirit as a friend; "doing good works without faith leads to death"; Native Americans: Great Spirit is loving father to all living creatures; Puritans: "Faith without works is death"; vengeful God. Bottom: Direct causes—Kieft had massacred innocent Native Americans who trusted him. Anne and her people were innocent and trusted Wampage. Indirect causes—Many whites considered Native Americans to be less-than-human and acted accordingly. The arrival of whites in America disrupted the Native American way of life.

The Man Who Would Not Change His Name

Discussion questions: 2. Caroline worried herself sick and died; Weldon was arrested for helping Caleb and died in prison; the Puritans in Boston had to deal with the Cavalier soldiers because the Puritans started a fight to help Caleb escape; the McDaniels family lost their home and the parents' lives.

Ticonderoga

Discussion questions: 1. Duncan agreed to give the stranger sanctuary, only later discovering that the man had killed his cousin. 3. They knew the fort's name but hadn't told Duncan.

Lydia Darragh

Discussion questions: 1. He and his troops were resting for the winter, planning a final strategy to defeat the American patriots. Lydia was a Quaker. Charles had joined the American Army. 2. When Lydia put up a fuss, the British agreed to let the family stay as long as the British could use the Darragh house for their meetings. The cause was aided because Lydia gained the opportunity to overhear information vital to the American Army. 5. "Anyone else."

Activity sheet: SURPRISE ATTACK BRITISH MARCH AT MIDNIGHT. Note: The code was created by substituting the letter C for A, D for B, E for C, and so on. Here are the letters of the alphabet and their equivalents in code:

Alphabet	Code	Alphabet	Code	Alphabet	Code
A	C	J	L	S	U
B	D	K	M	T	V
C	E	L	N	U	W
D	F	M	O	V	X
E	G	N	P	W	Y
F	H	O	Q	X	Z
G	I	P	R	Y	A
H	J	Q	S	Z	B
I	K	R	T		

Gone to War

Discussion questions: 3. Life in the cities was more refined: people lived in substantial homes and enjoyed the advantages of shops, schools, and churches. These were missing on the frontier, where mere survival was hard work.

Sacagawea's Story

Initiating activities: Identify on a map the area explored by Lewis and Clark—from St. Louis, up the Missouri River to its source in present-day Montana, across the Continental Divide, and down the Columbia River to the Pacific coast.

Discussion questions: 1. They needed horses to cross the mountains, and only the Shoshones had them. Without Sacagawea's knowledge of the Shoshone language and her connection with the tribe, the explorers probably wouldn't have been able to get the horses. 2. Answers will vary but should show students' knowledge of the location of wilderness areas that are not accessible by road. 3. The migratory nature of the Indians' lives and their way of fitting in with nature contrasted with whites' desire to own land, settle in one place, and tame the wilderness. 4. Sacagawea was captured by the Minnetarees, then gambled away to Charbonneau, who treated her like a slave and struck her.

Activity sheet: 1. Mississippi; 2. Michigan; 3. Massachusetts; 4. Minnesota; 5. Kentucky; 6. Alaska; 7. Wyoming; 8. Idaho; 9. Alabama. Famous Native American: Sacagawea.

A Love Story

Discussion questions: 1. Concha saw the San Francisco Bay, with forests on the opposite side. Today she would see a city skyline and the Golden Gate Bridge. 2. Father–daughter; citizen–country; romantic. 3. It was illegal to sell supplies to the Russians. Rezanoff showered the family with gifts and courted Concha.

Tsali: Cherokee Hero of the Smoky Mountains

Discussion questions: 1. Students might be surprised to learn that the Cherokee had schools and a legislative system and that they farmed. 2. Congress passed the resolution by one vote. It was reversed by the Supreme Court, headed by Chief Justice John Marshall. President Andrew Jackson decided to ignore the court's ruling. 3. The U.S. Army forced the Cherokees off their land and into stockades, where living conditions were miserable. Their property was stripped by the whites left behind, their farms raffled off to new owners. 4. He pushed and prodded Tsali's wife. 5. He thought it would prevent people from seeing Tsali and his sons as martyrs. His plan didn't work but instead called attention to Tsali's role as hero and martyr.

Tom Stowe

Discussion questions: 1. Tom was given his owner's last name. Emphasize that Henry Stowe was proud of Tom in the way one might be proud of a good hunting dog or a new car—as a possession, not as a human being. 3. His wife and child were back in Vicksburg. Tom did not trust white people in general, the way a beaten dog does not trust anyone. 4. Henry Stowe tried to rape Lucy, then sold her child out of spite and anger. He "watched Tom carefully" afterward, but there is no indication that he felt guilt—only that he didn't want to lose his possession. 6. Tom ended up in Canada, across from Buffalo, New York.

Westward Migration: Nancy Robbins's Story

Discussion questions: 1. She thought about bright sunshine and rich black soil and about her grandchildren growing up there. 2. Nancy was a positive thinker, and this helped others on the team. 4. Mrs. McGibney had the traditional view of that time, that Indians were "uncivilized heathens," whereas Mr. Steed was more sensitive, realizing that the Indians were simply trying to preserve their way of life.

Willie the Handcart Boy

Discussion questions: 1. People are exhausted; there is little food; Helen Blair and three other people have died during the night. 2. They seem to accept it calmly. 3. He feels important, determined to be strong. 4. Exposure to the icy water made his condition worse. 5. He hoped to find shelter. 6. They firmly believed they were traveling to Zion—they were compelled to try to reach it. They helped one another and prayed often.

Activity sheet: 1. F; 2. A; 3. O; 4. A; 5. O; 6. A; 7. A; 8. O; 9. A; 10. F.

Pioneering Spirit: The Story of Julia Archibald Holmes

Initiating activity: In colonial times only land-owning white males could vote. Some conservatives today feel that only taxpayers should vote. Propose this possibility to students for a lively debate.

Discussion questions: 2. The Archibalds offered their home as a stop on the Underground Railroad.

Why Lincoln Grew a Beard

Discussion questions: 1. Women could not vote in 1860. 3. The modern White House receives thousands of letters every day, most of which are answered by staff members and never seen by the president. 5. There was no television, and even photography was in its early stages. Apparently the change in Lincoln's appearance had not been mentioned in the newspapers. 6. Antislavery groups supported him, whereas proslavery groups and advocates of states' rights considered him an enemy of their way of life. Staunch abolitionists, however, found him "too mild."

Activity sheet: The following did not exist: 3, 7, 9, 10, 13, 14, 15, 18, 19, 21, 22, 25, 26, 27, 28, 32, 33, 34, 35.

A Cold Night

Discussion questions: 1. Rosecrans hoped to take Murfreesboro and then Chattanooga. Bragg hoped to drive the Union Army out of Nashville. 2. Bragg's failure to attack on January 1 may have been the major factor contributing to the Union victory. 3. Point out the line "He had died on the spot where he lay . . . or so it seemed" on page 74 of *Many Voices*. 6. Students could ask a doctor or conduct research on head injuries to find out if receiving a bullet through the skull is always immediately fatal.

The Story of Wilmer McLean

Discussion questions: 2. Wilmer's "sinking feeling" warns him to round up his cows and tell his wife and children to go inside. 3. His family's safety. 4. People gawk at highway accidents; seem to enjoy boxing, hockey, wrestling, and football partly for the violence; watch shows such as *Rescue 911* to see people narrowly escape death; are fascinated by gory murder cases. 5. The deaths on both sides sadden Wilmer to the point of tears. 7. The issues of states' rights and slavery were apparently not vitally important to Wilmer; he simply wanted to keep his family safe and farm his land in peace.

The Cardiff Giant

Questions are open-ended.

Wild Bill Hickok in Springfield

Discussion questions: 1. Tutt wanted the watch because it meant a lot to Hickok. 2. He fired first. Students may enjoy discussing whether Tutt had any chance. He might have thought that firing first was the only chance he had. 3. By 1873 Springfield had a city marshal, streetlights, and a justice of the peace. 4. With such a small and insubstantial jail, the town must have been a pretty peaceful place most of the time. 5. Stokes was older, and Hickok was being respectful as well as familiar.

Inspector Walsh and Sitting Bull

Discussion questions: 1. Both groups rode horses and traveled in remote areas that were unsettled. The U.S. Cavalry was not noted for its fairness to Indians. "Shoot first, think later" might have been its motto, whereas that of the NWMP would have been the opposite. The Sioux were grateful for the attitude the NWMP showed toward them.

Aunt Clara Brown

Discussion questions: 5. Mr. Smith bought Richard, and Richard and Clara married. The family was kept together until after Mr. Smith's death, at which point others stepped in and devastated their lives. 6. She finally had personal freedom. She attended a black church and made a best friend.

Launching a Scientist:
Robert Goddard's First Attempt at Rocketry

Discussion questions: 1. Percy stands for the doubters who have always said to scientists, "It can't be done." People laughed at Columbus, Copernicus, Thomas Edison, and Bill

Gates, who predicted the popularity of the personal computer. 2. Birds have many hollow bones, which reduce their body weight and provide storage for air; birds' wings provide propulsion and lift. Birds glide on air currents once they are airborne.

The Year of the Turnip in Oklahoma

Discussion questions: 1. They had been itinerant tenant farmers and had found it difficult to get ahead. 3. Biscuits: Bread and cereal. Milk: Dairy. Pickles: Vegetable and fruit.

Activity sheet: Sample menus (students' menus may vary, but total of items should be no more than $12): Breakfasts: Wheat flakes with milk, toast and jelly, grapefruit; wheat flakes with milk, corn muffins, grapefruit. Lunches: Egg-salad sandwich, apple, carrot sticks, milk; peanut-butter-and-jelly sandwich, apple, carrot sticks, milk. Dinners: Pinto beans and rice, corn muffins, lettuce salad, milk; scrambled eggs, buttered toast, canned tomatoes, milk. Snacks: Carrot sticks, apple with peanut butter, rice.

Zayde's Trunk

Discussion questions: 2. Cuba, Serbia, Bosnia, Iraq, Iran—anywhere there is war or totalitarian rule. 3. A bar mitzvah (literally "son commandment") is often followed by elaborate parties with many guests to celebrate a young man's adulthood and give him gifts. Today Conservative, Reform, and Reconstructionist Jews hold bas or bat mitzvahs for girls, but in Itzi's day this was not the case. 4. The immigrants provided plenty of cheap labor for the factories as well as occupants for run-down tenements. Illegal aliens today are often employed at below-minimum-wage jobs. 5. Itzi's entrepreneurial spirit should be noted.

Activity sheet: 1. Shlep; 2. cockamamie; 3. kibbitz; 4. glitch; 5. strictly from hunger; 6. mazel tov; 7. shlemiel; 8. klutz; 9. nosh, bagel.

Scott Joplin: Master of Ragtime

Discussion questions: 1. Sheet music. Scott Joplin learned musical notation so he could write his songs down for anyone to play. 4. Some examples: Aretha Franklin, Whitney Houston, Diana Ross. 5. Sample answers: CD players, boom boxes, video games, computers, movies, television, videos, theme parks.

Answers to crossword puzzle are on page 79.

The Courage of Ed Pulaski

Discussion questions: 2. Everyone had a part to play, and all the men depended on one another for survival. 5. The firefighting tool he invented, an ax-hoe combination, is called a Pulaski.

The Laundry Man Who Overthrew the Qing Dynasty

Questions are open-ended.

Stagecoach Mary

Questions are open-ended.

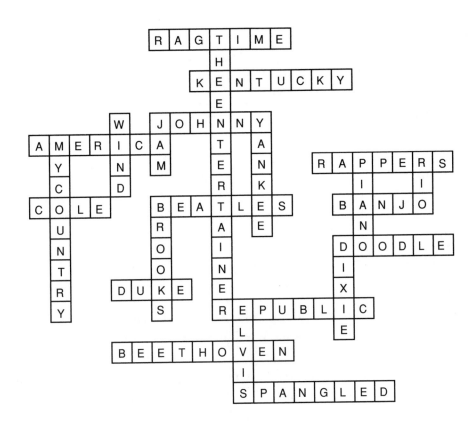

The Horse That Went to War

Questions are open-ended. Students may have written letters or sent packages to soldiers who served in the Gulf War, and you might connect Evelyn's war effort with theirs.

Say Goodbye to Papa: The Regina Sinreich Barton Story

Initiating activities: According to the "salad bowl" view, Americans of different nationalities are mixed together, but each nationality's ethnic flavor remains separate. The existence of predominantly African-American ghettos and ethnic enclaves such as Chinatown, Little Italy, Little Poland, and so on in many large cities provides evidence that this may be the case. An interesting discussion may ensue when students are asked just how Americanized immigrants should become.

   Discussion questions: 2. Point out the attempts of Cubans and Haitians to sail to Florida on rickety rafts—most knowing that they will be picked up by U.S. officials before they get very far. Mexican illegal immigrants often walk across the border. Some swim across the Rio Grande River.

Rider on an Orphan Train

Discussion questions: 1. Ideally children stayed with siblings and were adopted by loving families who treated them as their own. The worst scenario would be separation from siblings and being taken in by families who would treat the orphans as little more than slaves.

The Herring Shed

Questions are open-ended.

Rosie the Riveter

Discussion questions: 1. The "Rosies" proved that women could work just as efficiently as men and still accomplish what had to be done at home.

Such Things to Write About

Questions are open-ended.

The Garbage Story

Questions are open-ended.

An Orange

Questions are open-ended.

Snapshot, 1944

Discussion questions: 1. The painful irony of this story is that the dead son whose funeral is the subject of the snapshot died as an American soldier, while his family were interned in a relocation camp because they were Japanese—"the enemy."

Activity sheet: Note: Explain that the Japanese do not use the same alphabet we do and that the words listed are written with our alphabet in a way that approximates Japanese pronunciations. 1. F; 2. I; 3. P; 4. R; 5. K; 6. C; 7. L; 8. G; 9. M; 10. H; 11. D; 12. Q; 13. T; 14. B; 15. U; 16. S; 17. N; 18. O; 19. J; 20. E; 21. A.

Precious Freedom

Questions are open-ended.

Resources

Anne Hutchinson

IlgenFritz, Elizabeth, *Anne Hutchinson*, Chelsea House, 1991

Jacobs, William Jay, *Roger Williams*, Watts, 1975

Keehn, Sally, *I Am Regina*, Philomel, 1991

Locker, Thomas, *The Land of Gray Wolf*, Dial, 1991

Speare, Elizabeth George, *The Witch of Blackbird Pond*, Houghton Mifflin, 1958

—, *Calico Captive*, Houghton Mifflin, 1957

The Man Who Would Not Change His Name

Kaplan, Lawrence, *Oliver Cromwell*, Chelsea House, 1986

Linington, Elizabeth, *The Kingbreaker*, Doubleday, 1958

Ticonderoga

Cohen, Daniel, *Ghostly Tales of Love and Revenge*, Putnam, 1992

Cooper, James Fenimore, *The Last of the Mohicans* (many editions)

Graymont, Barbara, *The Iroquois*, University of Oklahoma Press, 1991

Morris, Richard Brandon, *The Indian Wars*, Lerner, 1985

Lydia Darragh

Anticaglia, Elizabeth, *Heroines of '76*, Walker, 1975

Bakeless, Katherine, and John Bakeless, *Spies of the Revolution*, Lippincott, 1962

Clapp, Patricia, *I'm Deborah Sampson: A Soldier in the War of the Revolution*, Lothrop, Lee & Shepard, 1977

Haynes, Betsy, *Spies on the Devil's Belt*, Nelson, 1974

O'Dell, Scott, *Sarah Bishop*, Houghton Mifflin, 1980

Gone to War

Collier, James, *My Brother Sam Is Dead*, Four Winds, 1985

Dalgliesh, Alice, *The Courage of Sarah Noble*, Aladdin, 1991

Forbes, Esther, *Johnny Tremain*, Houghton Mifflin, 1943

Meltzer, Milton, editor, *The American Revolutionaries: A History in Their Own Words, 1750–1800*, Crowell, 1987

Sacagawea's Story

Blumberg, Rhoda, *The Incredible Journey of Lewis and Clark*, Lothrop, Lee & Shepard, 1987

Fradin, Dennis B., *The Shoshoni*, Childrens Press, 1988

Freedman, Russell, *An Indian Winter*, Holiday House, 1992

O'Dell, Scott, *Streams to the River, River to the Sea: A Novel of Sacagawea*, Houghton Mifflin, 1986

Seymour, Flora W., *Sacagawea: American Pathfinder*, Aladdin, 1991

A Love Story

Baker, Betty, *The Dunderhead War*, Harper, 1967

Parker, F. M., *The Far Battleground*, New American Library, 1988

Pearsall, Robert, and Ursula Spier Erickson, editors, *The Californians: Writings of Their Past and Present*, Hesperian House, 1961

Pierce, Richard A., editor, *Russia in North America*, Limestone, 1990

Tsali: Cherokee Hero
Of the Smoky Mountains

Claro, Nicole, *The Cherokee Indians*, Chelsea House, 1992

Ehle, John, *Trail of Tears: The Rise and Fall of the Cherokee Nation*, Doubleday, 1988

Jones, Jayne Clark, *The American Indians in America*, Lerner, 1991

Klausner, Janet, *Sequoyah's Gift: A Portrait of the Cherokee Leader*, HarperCollins, 1993

Roth, Susan L., *Kanahena: A Cherokee Story*, St. Martin's, 1988

Tom Stowe

Armstrong, Jennifer, *Steal Away*, Orchard Books, 1992

Hamilton, Virginia, *Anthony Burns: The Defeat and Triumph of a Fugitive Slave*, Knopf, 1988

Lester, Julius, *To Be a Slave*, Dial, 1968

Rappaport, Doreen, *Escape From Slavery: Five Journeys to Freedom*, HarperCollins, 1991

Westward Migration:
Nancy Robbins's Story

Conrad, Pam, *Prairie Songs*, Harper & Row, 1985

Morrow, Honore, *On to Oregon*, Beech Tree, 1991

Wexler, Sanford, editor, *Westward Expansion: An Eyewitness History*, Facts on File, 1991

Eide, Ingvard Henry, *Oregon Trail*, Rand McNally, 1973

Willie the Handcart Boy

Hafen, Le Roy R., and Ann W. Hafen, *Handcarts to Zion*, University of Nebraska Press, 1992

Kimball, Stanley B., *Mormon Pioneer National Historic Trail*, U.S. Department of the Interior, National Park Service, 1991

Pioneering Spirit: The Story
Of Julia Archibald Holmes

Blumberg, Rhoda, *Bloomers!*, Bradbury, 1993

Jacobs, William, *Mother, Aunt Susan and Me: The First Fight for Women's Rights*, Coward, McCann & Geoghegan, 1979

Lasky, Kathryn, *Beyond the Divide*, Macmillan, 1983

Scott, Jack Denton, and Ozzie Sweet, *Return of the Buffalo*, Putnam, 1976

Why Lincoln Grew a Beard

Freedman, Russell, *Lincoln: A Photobiography*, Clarion, 1987

A Cold Night

Cohen, Daniel, *The Restless Dead: Ghostly Tales From Around the World*, Dodd, Mead, 1984

Hunt, Irene, *Across Five Aprils*, Silver Burdett, 1993

Keith, Harold, *Rifles for Watie*, Crowell, 1957

Stevens, Bryna, *Frank Thompson: Her Civil War Story*, Macmillan, 1992

The Story of Wilmer McLean

Beatty, Patricia, *Be Ever Hopeful, Hannalee*, Morrow, 1988

St. George, Judith, *Mason and Dixon's Line of Fire*, Putnam, 1991

The Cardiff Giant

Saunders, Richard, *The World's Greatest Hoaxes*, Playboy, 1980

Wild Bill Hickok in Springfield

Faber, Doris, *Calamity Jane: Her Life and Her Legend*, Houghton Mifflin, 1992

Freedman, Russell, *Children of the Wild West*, Clarion, 1983

Greer, Gery, *Max and Me and the Wild West*, Harcourt Brace Jovanovich, 1988

Portis, Charles, *True Grit*, Simon & Schuster, 1968

Stevenson, Augusta, *Buffalo Bill: Frontier Daredevil*, Aladdin, 1991

Inspector Walsh and Sitting Bull

Charters, Dean, *Mountie, 1873-1973: A Golden Treasury of Those Early Years*, Collier-Macmillan Canada, 1973

Lunn, Janet, and Christopher Moore, *The Story of Canada*, Lester Publishing and Key Porter Books, 1992

MacLeod, R. C., *The Mounties: Focus on History Series*, Grolier, 1985

McGaw, Jessie Brewer, *Chief Red Horse Tells About Custer: The Battle of the Little Bighorn*, Elsevier/Nelson, 1981

Aunt Clara Brown

Johnson, Dolores, *Now Let Me Fly: The Story of a Slave Family*, Macmillan, 1993

Lyons, Mary, *Letters From a Slave Girl: The Story of Harriet Jacobs*, Scribner, 1992

Walker, Margaret, *Jubilee*, Houghton Mifflin, 1966

Launching a Scientist: Robert Goddard's First Attempt at Rocketry

Branley, Franklyn M., *Gravity Is a Mystery*, Crowell, 1986

Holland, Peter, *Amazing Models: Gravity Power*, Tab, 1990

Zubrowski, Bernie, *Balloons: Building and Experimenting With Inflatable Toys*, Morrow, 1990

The Year of the Turnip In Oklahoma

Antle, Nancy, *Beautiful Land: A Story of the Oklahoma Land Rush*, Viking, 1994

Hancock, Mary A., *The Thundering Prairie*, Macrae Smith, 1969

Keith, Harold, *The Obstinate Land*, Crowell, 1977

Zayde's Trunk

Anderson, Kelly C., *Immigration*, Lucent, 1993

Drucker, Malka, *Celebrating Life: Jewish Rites of Passage*, Holiday House, 1984

Fisher, Leonard E., *A Russian Farewell*, Four Winds, 1980

Matas, Carol, *Sworn Enemies*, Bantam, 1993

Sevela, Efraim, *Why There Is No Heaven on Earth*, Harper & Row, 1982

Telushkin, Joseph, *Jewish Literacy: The Most Important Things to Know About the Jewish Religion, Its People, and Its History*, Morrow, 1991

Scott Joplin: Master of Ragtime

Berlin, Edward A., *Ragtime: A Musical and Cultural History*, University of California Press, 1980

Haskins, James, and Kathleen Benson, *Scott Joplin*, Doubleday, 1978

The Courage of Ed Pulaski

Goddard, Kenneth W., *Wildfire*, Forge, 1994

Lawter, William Jr., *Smokey Bear 20252: A Biography*, Lindsay Smith, 1994

Maclean, Norman, *Young Men and Fire*, Hall, 1993

Vogt, Gregory, *Forests on Fire: The Fight to Save Our Trees*, Watts, 1990

White, Robb, *Fire Storm*, Doubleday, 1979

The Laundry Man Who Overthrew the Qing Dynasty

Neville, Emily C., *The China Year*, HarperCollins, 1991

Perl, Lila, *Red Star and Green Dragon: Looking at New China*, Morrow, 1983

Yep, Laurence, *The Rainbow People*, Harper & Row, 1989

Stagecoach Mary

Adams, Samuel H., *The Pony Express*, Random House, 1950

McNeese, Tim, *Conestogas and Stagecoaches*, Crestwood House, 1993

Roth, Harold, *First Class! The Postal System in Action*, Pantheon, 1983

The Horse That Went to War

Facklam, Margery, *Who Harnessed the Horse? The Story of Animal Domestication*, Little, Brown, 1992

Skurzynski, Gloria, *Goodbye, Billy Radish*, Bradbury, 1992

Ventura, Piero, *Man and the Horse*, Putnam, 1982

Say Goodbye to Papa: The Regina Sinreich Barton Story

Fisher, Leonard E., *Ellis Island: Gateway to the New World*, Holiday House, 1986

Freedman, Russell, *Immigrant Kids*, Dutton, 1980

Koral, April, *An Album of the Great Wave of Immigration*, Watts, 1992

Stein, R. Conrad, *Ellis Island*, Childrens Press, 1992

Rider on an Orphan Train

Ball, Zachary, *North to Abilene*, Holiday House, 1960

Coleman, Lonnie, *Orphan Jim*, Doubleday, 1975

Warren, Andrea, *The Orphan Train: One Rider's Story*, Houghton Mifflin, 1995

The Herring Shed

McCutcheon, Elsie, *Summer of the Zeppelin*, Farrar, Straus & Giroux, 1985

Mukerji, Dhan Gopal, *Gay-Neck: The Story of a Pigeon*, Dutton, 1968

Trumbo, Dalton, *Johnny Got His Gun*, Lippincott, 1939

Rosie the Riveter

Fisher, Leonard E., *The Factories*, Holiday House, 1979

Frank, Miriam, Marilyn Ziebarth, and Connie Field, *The Life and Times of Rosie the Riveter: The Story of Three Million Working Women During World War II*, Clarity Educational Productions, 1982

Gluck, Sherna Berger, *Rosie the Riveter Revisited: Women, the War, and Social Change*, New American Library, 1988

McNeer, May, *Bloomsday for Maggie*, Houghton Mifflin, 1976

Miles, Betty, *The Real Me*, Knopf, 1974

Such Things to Write About

Degens, T., *The Visit*, Viking, 1982

Kerr, M. E., *Gentlehands*, Harper & Row, 1978

Mazer, Harry, *The Last Mission*, Delacorte, 1979

Orlev, Uri, *The Island on Bird Street*, Houghton Mifflin, 1984

Poynter, Margaret, *A Time Too Swift*, Atheneum, 1990

The Garbage Story

Levine, Ellen, *Freedom's Children: Young Civil Rights Activists Tell Their Own Stories*, Thorndike, 1993

Harrington, Michael, *The Other America: Poverty in the United States*, Penguin, 1992

Haskins, James, *The March on Washington*, HarperCollins, 1993

Baldwin, James, *Notes of a Native Son*, Beacon, 1990

An Orange

Levoy, Myron, *Alan and Naomi*, Harper & Row, 1977

Lowry, Lois, *Number the Stars*, Houghton Mifflin, 1989

Meltzer, Milton, *Never to Forget: The Jews of the Holocaust*, Harper & Row, 1976

Rogasky, Barbara, *Smoke and Ashes: The Story of the Holocaust*, Holiday House, 1988

Snapshot, 1944

Houston, Jeanne Wakatsuki, and James D. Houston, *Farewell to Manzanar: A True Story of Japanese American Experience During and After the World War II Internment*, Houghton Mifflin, 1973

Means, Florence C., *The Moved-Outers*, Walker, 1992

Uchida, Yoshiko, *The Invisible Thread: An Autobiography*, Messner, 1991

—, *Journey to Topaz: A Story of the Japanese-American Evacuation*, Scribner, 1971

Precious Freedom

Fisher, Leonard E., *A Russian Farewell,* Four Winds, 1980

Moskin, Marietta, *Waiting for Mama*, Coward, McCann & Geoghegan, 1975

Sachs, Marilyn, *Call Me Ruth*, Doubleday, 1982